James
Dean
a biography

D1390191

James Dean

a biography

John Howlett

Plexus, London

For Stephen Hamilton
who might have written this book

Published by Plexus Publishing Limited
55a Clapham Common Southside
London SW4 9BX
First Printing 1997

British Library Cataloguing in Publication Data
Howlett, John, 1940-
    James Dean: a biography. - Rev. and updated ed.
    1.Dean, James, 1931-1955 2.Motion picture
    actors and actresses - United States - Biography
    I.Title
    791.4'3'028'092

    ISBN 0 85965 243 2

Printed in Great Britain by J.W. Arrowsmith
Designed by Mitchell Associates

Acknowledgements

The hysteria that followed James Dean's death
made grotesque and impossible demands on
his family, his friends and the people who had
worked with him. Consequently there was an
understandable reluctance among many of
them to reopen a subject that had plagued
them at the time. Material for the first edition
of this book was not easy to obtain and I am
particularly grateful for the help that was
given and my special thanks to all those who
did communicate – in particular Nick Ray,
Natalie Wood and Elia Kazan – and no hard
feelings towards those who politely declined.
    I would like to express my thanks to
William Bast for his book *James Dean*
(Ballantine Books, 1956) which had been
particularly helpful to me in my initial
research. My thanks also to the staff at the
British Film Institute book library for their
interest and assistance; to Ray Connolly for
giving me access to his own interviews; to Leo
Wilder and Warner Brothers for their co-
operation over photographs and in making
available the James Dean films; to Nigel
Mallinson, Connie Bessie, Mike Kaplan, Frank
Radcliffe, Joe Massot, Marianne Alexandre,
Douglas Gibbons and Thaddeus O'Sullivan for
their help in obtaining photographs,
interviews, facts, and loaning material; to
Diana Matias for the translations; to Richard
Perrin for the loan of his posters; to Al Reuter
for the loan of his stills. The photographs and
stills illustrating this book are by courtesy of
Warner Brothers, the National Film Archive
(London), and Magnum Photos (the John
Hillelson Agency). It has not been possible in
all cases to trace the copyright sources, and my
publishers would be glad to hear from any
such unacknowledged copyright holders.
    For this second edition I should like to draw
attention to the more recent biographies listed
in the bibliography, in particular Donald
Spoto's *Rebel: The Life and Legend of James Dean*,
Paul Alexander's *James Dean – Boulevard of
Broken Dreams*, Val Holley's *James Dean – The
Biography*, Ronald Martinetti's *The James Dean
Story* and Warner Brothers' *James Dean – Behind
the Scene*. A reassessment of the James Dean
films forty years on could not have been
achieved without the observations of a new
generation. I was surprised that my daughters
should have identified with and enjoyed the
three films as much as they did – and continue
to do. I am grateful for their observations and
those of their friends.
    Finally my tribute and thanks to three
people without whom this book would never
have been written: to Terence Porter for
conceiving the project; David Sherwin for
suggesting me as author; and Sandra Wake for
her inexhaustible patience and help
throughout research and writing of both the
original edition and this revised version.

John Howlett

Contents

Preface

If a man can bridge the gap between life and
death, I mean, if he can live on after he's died,
then maybe he was a great man.

James Dean

JAMES DEAN died at the age of 24, fulfilling his own premonition of an early death. He
was killed in a Porsche Spyder on his way to compete in a race meeting, victim of a
banal traffic accident. He had been working in Hollywood for only sixteen months and
just one of his three films had so far been released. Yet that one film had already
established him as a major star. Death would now make him the cult figure of his and
following generations and provoke a hysteria unparalleled since the time of Rudolph
Valentino. It was a legend that became briefly hideous: a necromantic, necrophagous and,
for some, highly profitable frenzy. The very sickness of the cult should have killed his
name and reputation. Yet they survived, his face and manner images to dominate the
genesis of pop culture in the 1960s. Elvis Presley, Buddy Holly, Little Richard, the Everly
Brothers, Eddie Cochran, Bob Dylan: they all belonged among those who idolised Jimmy
Dean. It was as though he had pushed open the door for them.

They were not articulate, the post-war adolescents of the mid-fifties. They were
scarcely conscious of themselves as an entity. The Kerouac-style 'beats' and the rock and
roll *aficionados* were still minorities. The majority, truly silent, had no sub-culture of their
own in which to hide, or through which to express their hopes and frustrations. The
cinema was their only refuge and Hollywood stories their only escape. The moment James
Dean appeared on that screen in front of them – angry, dishevelled, hurt, unsophisticated,
androgynously beautiful – their response was immediate.

He appealed equally to girls and to boys, to men and women and when his first film,
East of Eden, was released in March 1955, young people all over the world recognised
themselves in his portrayal of lost adolescence. He became, literally overnight, a superstar.
The title of his second film, released two weeks after his death, exactly defined his image
and status: *Rebel Without a Cause.*

He died leaving that image uncompromised in any of his three roles. He had not
wandered, as an actor must, beyond self-reality. He had portrayed himself, and the
traumas and style of his life made the identification genuine. He had also quite
consciously played to his image. 'How can I lose?' he told a friend. 'In one hand I got
Marlon Brando yelling "Fuck you all"; in the other, Montgomery Clift asking "Please
help me".'

Revelations continue to be claimed and denied about his private life and how he whored his way to success on the casting couches of homosexual Hollywood and Manhattan. As with any subject of posthumous biography, the whole truth belongs only with him. Speculation about his sexuality had started already during his own short lifetime and was for many of his closer friends a forbidden subject after his death. Yet that very ambiguity with his lost boy looks would make him the ultimate bisexual icon for each succeeding generation.

Forty years later he is either half-remembered as an 'insufferable little jerk' or still revered as a distant myth, puzzled over by generations that recognise the image but hardly know who he is. He appeared to Eisenhower's paternalistic America of the 1950s as ill-mannered, petulant, selfish – and has regularly been dismissed in much the same language ever since. What cannot be dismissed so easily is the astonishing effect his behavioural acting had on young audiences and how, for better or for worse, that effect gave image and identity to the youth cultures about to liberate the western world. Marlon Brando, it was said, changed the way actors acted; James Dean changed the way people behaved.

Halfway between then and now, in 1972 the Andy Warhol *Interview* reassessed the legend, defined his achievement and identified the nostalgia that has kept the myth alive. Their words are still apposite:

> James Dean made just three pictures, but even if he had made only one he would still be the greatest male star of the '50s. The pictures are *East of Eden, Rebel Without a Cause, Giant.* Just the titles evoke epic visions, and all three films live up to their titles, constituting a three part heroic poem on atomic age youth, its beauties and its obsessions... James Dean was the perfect embodiment of an eternal struggle. It might be innocence struggling with experience, youth with age, or man with his image. But in every aspect his struggle was a mirror to a generation of rebels without a cause. His anguish was exquisitely genuine on and off the screen; his moments of joy were rare and precious. He is not our hero because he was perfect, but because he perfectly represented the damaged but beautiful soul of our time...

An actor must interpret life and in order to do so he must be willing to accept all experiences that life has to offer. In fact he must seek out more of life than life puts at his feet. In the short span of his lifetime an actor must learn all there is to know, experience all there is to experience, or approach that state as closely as possible. He must be superhuman in his efforts to store away in the warehouse of his subconscious everything that he might be called upon to use in the expression of his art. Nothing should be more important to the artist than life and the living of it, not even the ego. To grasp the full significance of life is the actor's duty; to interpret it his problem; and to express it his dedication... Being an actor is the loneliest thing in the world. You're all alone with your concentration and imagination, and that's all you have. Being an actor isn't easy. Being a man is even harder. I want to be both before I'm done.

James Dean

1. Orphan

I told him straight one evening: 'Your mother's never coming home again.' All he did was stare at me.

Winton Dean

JAMES BYRON DEAN was born on 8 February 1931, at the Green Gables Apartments on East Fourth Street, in the small industrial town of Marion, fifty miles north of Indianapolis, his mother giving him the christian name of a family friend and the family name of her favourite poet, Lord Byron.

The choice of eponym surprised no one in her family. Mildred Wilson had been brought up by her own parents with a love of poetry and music and a vision of worlds beyond their mid-west farming background. A passionate romance and an unexpected pregnancy had forced her to settle for the attainable in her own life, but she had greater ambitions for her son. However unplanned, marriage had now taken her out of farming and into the classless gentility of small town suburbia: her lover and now husband, Winton Dean, was a dental mechanic in the respectable and safe employ of the Federal Government, a steady job with a regular salary, important security in those years of uncertainty. And through this security Mildred Dean intended to give her son the opportunities she had never known.

The vivacious, good-looking, young mother deliberately set about creating the atmosphere and conditions in which she believed prodigy would develop. She read her son poetry, played to him on the piano, took him for long walks into the country. When he was old enough to sustain interest in a game, they built a toy theatre together, an up-turned cardboard box pinned with curtains, in which they acted out stories and make-believe with puppets and dolls. And as soon as the little boy was strong enough to hold it, Mildred bought him a child's violin, sending him to lessons in the town, encouraging a musical talent that proved at the time to be non-existent.

Mother and son were sharing an almost secretive life of their own, with games and rituals into which the father rarely intruded. At night young Jimmy would write notes or draw pictures for his mother, describing something he particularly wanted to do, or to possess. He would leave the note under his pillow and if his request was at all feasible Mildred Dean would do her best to fulfil it. There were those on both sides of the family who criticised her. They felt the boy was growing up too sheltered and over-indulged. Certainly he was teased by his cousins for the poetry-reading and the violin lessons and when the time came for him to start school he already felt himself set apart from the other

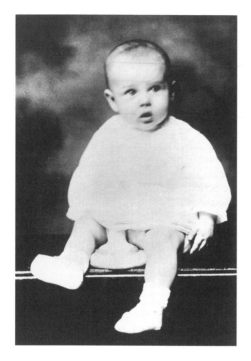

Jimmy growing up.

Jimmy with his mother and father, Mildred and Winton Dean.

children. It was a sense of detachment that would stay with him until his death, partly through circumstances, partly as a result of this childhood involvement with his mother's ambition for achievement and success.

When Jimmy was six years old his father was transferred from Indiana to a job at the Sawtelle Veterans' Administration Hospital in Los Angeles – an attempt, perhaps, to breathe new life into a not altogether successful marriage. The family moved three thousand miles across the continent, into a small house in Santa Monica, and after the summer vacation Jimmy was enrolled in the Brentwood Public School, a short bus ride from Burbank and the Sunset Boulevard where his mother's ambition would be one day dramatically, if briefly, fulfilled.

Teachers at the Brentwood School remembered him as a shy young boy who had great difficulty in making friends. He was quick and bright in the classroom but a natural target for ridicule with his violin-case, his dancing lessons and his pretentious middle name. 'James Byron', the boys called him, and ignored his family nickname, 'Deanie'.

The move away from family and friends in Indiana placed an even greater emphasis on the already close relationship between mother and son. Neither of them seemed to make any close relationships in Santa Monica and when his mother fell ill during his eighth and ninth years, the young boy was profoundly disturbed by what appeared to him as distance and change in her attitude towards him. To some visiting relatives in 1939, Mildred Dean seemed tired and dispirited; the effect, they thought, of the move to the west coast climate. In fact Mildred was seriously ill and by the time cancer of the breast had been diagnosed, her condition was declining too rapidly for treatment. It was a period of confusion and fear for the boy, his immediate reaction to her illness being resentment and even anger. Grief and incomprehension came later as he watched her beauty, energy, and resilience fade away.

Incomprehension was just as overpowering for Winton Dean. It was the first time father and son had been left alone together and during their visits to the hospital in the later stages of her illness, the father attempted to convey to the young boy the inevitability of his mother's death: 'I tried to get it across to him, to prepare him in some way, but he just didn't seem to take it in. I told him straight one evening: "Your mother's never coming home again." All he did was stare at me.'

Perhaps it was natural if the boy transferred some of his fear and resentment towards the father. Instead of coming together through the tragedy, the two of them were growing apart, and this process – avoidable or not, we cannot know – was to have a decisive effect on the next ten years of Dean's life.

Winton Dean had asked his mother, Emma Dean, to travel out from Indiana to look after them during the last weeks of his wife's illness. The hospital bills and his mother's fare exhausted the family funds. Even the car had to be sold and when the Wilson family asked him to send Mildred home to Indiana for burial, Winton Dean could not afford to make the journey himself. His mother now suggested taking the boy back with her, to live with Winton's sister and brother-in-law, Ortense and Marcus, in Fairmount.

Bewildered and unsure of himself, Winton Dean agreed that his son might be better cared for on an Indiana farm than in an empty house in the Los Angeles suburbs. Right or wrong, the decision was almost certainly a direct result of the boy's estrangement during the last stages of his mother's illness. The prospect of coping with his son's silent withdrawal

On the farm: first steps in the pole vault; gardening with Marcus junior.

Jimmy's grandma, Emma Dean.

Jimmy's grandpa, Charlie Dean.

was too much for the father and in the space of a day the boy had lost, to all intents and purposes, both his parents. Winton Dean would never quite come to terms with what he had done. None of Dean's friends or colleagues who later met the father seemed able to relate to him in any positive way and however often they saw each other during the next sixteen years, communication between father and son would never be satisfactorily restored.

Jimmy was nine years old when he said goodbye to his father and rode home to Indiana with his grandmother, his mother's sealed coffin in the luggage-van. The boy would walk down the train at each station stop to check the coffin. No one remembers him crying very much. 'He shut it all inside him,' a cousin said. 'The only person he could ever have talked about it with was lying there in the casket.'

The body rested with relatives while the funeral was arranged, and it is said that late one night the boy crept downstairs to where the coffin was lying and took the ribbon from one of the wreaths. According to his aunt he kept the ribbon neatly folded under his pillow for months afterwards.

The Winslow farm is situated on the outskirts of the small agricultural town of Fairmount, ten miles to the south of Dean's birthplace in Marion, the house white-boarded and roomy, the yard always full of animals, the fields beyond undulating and varied, crossed by the Back Creek stream. Jimmy's cousin Joan was only a few years older than he, and in addition to his uncle and aunt, Marcus and Ortense Winslow, the grandparents Charlie and Emma Dean lived only a short distance away in the middle of town. It was a friendly, informal, family atmosphere and the Quaker background, common to both the Deans and the Winslows, intruded with only marginal severity on Jimmy's new way of life.

But it was a long time before the boy relaxed into his new environment – maybe as long as the months it took the children at the Fairmount School to forget him as 'the poor orphan' and accept him instead as Joan Winslow's kid brother. For a while he resisted any attempt to draw him out of his self-absorption and his isolated sense of grief and grievance. For the rest of his life Dean, and anyone who had the misfortune to be with him at the time, would be tormented by these oppressive moods of withdrawal and there was little anyone could do to break their spell.

The Winslows distracted him with the routines of farm life. Before his tenth birthday Uncle Marcus had taught him how to drive and service the tractor, how to look after the livestock, how best to stalk and shoot the rats in the farmyard or the rabbits on the land. For his tenth birthday they gave him a horse, on condition that he look after it himself, and, until he was old enough to take motorbikes onto the public highways of Grant County, the tractor, the horse, and the gun gave him the freedom of the Winslows' 440 acres of Indiana countryside.

The Winslows worked their farm without regular help and the daily and seasonal chores became part of Dean's life. In an interview with columnist Hedda Hopper fifteen years later, a more sophisticated young man recalled those early days helping – and skiving – on his uncle's land: 'This was a real farm and I worked like crazy as long as someone was watching me. Forty acres of oats made a huge stage and when the audience left I took a nap and nothing got ploughed or harrowed. Then I met a friend who lived over in Marion and he taught me how to wrestle and kill cats, and other things boys do behind barns. And I began to live.'

At junior school they couldn't quite figure him out. His grades were too high and until he entered senior school he was always ahead of his year. When his grades fell off he argued that it was on account of trying to do too much: 'Why did God put all these things here for us to be interested in?'

In his twelfth year Dean had to undergo a further period of emotional adjustment with the arrival of young Marc in the Winslow family. A baby son, long awaited by Marcus and Ortense, diverted attention away from Jimmy and reminded him that while he had come to call his aunt and uncle 'mom and dad', he had less right to their time and affection than their own two children. Not that there was any change in their attitude towards him. The change was in himself, and noticed only by his teacher and grandparents. The birth of his young cousin emphasised the direction of his emotional life: one more degree of isolation and self-sufficiency; and the beginnings of self-assertion.

An early result of self-assertion was the arrival of Dean's first motorbike – a motorised cycle called a 'Whizzer', hardly fast enough to endanger life or limb, but good enough for trick-riding round the farm. Even at this age he had a predisposition for speed and brinkmanship, ignoring his handicap of bad short-sight. On the farm he was never content unless he ended a day's work swinging tractor and trailer through the yard gates or into the barn at speed, and at the narrowest possible angle. He experimented for hours on a trapeze his uncle had built for him, until he finally over-reached himself and smashed his front teeth in a fall (thereafter he had to wear a bridge with two false teeth). So now with his 'Whizzer', he rode it hard as though breaking in a young horse, to find its limits of speed and adhesion. 'I used to go out for the cows on the motorcycle,' he told Hedda Hopper. 'Scared the hell out of them. They'd get to running and their udders would start swinging, and they'd lose a quart of milk.' Apart from the milk, his antics also cost him four pairs of new spectacles in as many weeks. The family was finally persuaded that a real motorbike might be less costly and dangerous.

It was the local Wesleyan Minister who had first encouraged Dean's passion for 'hazard' and now introduced him not only to the sensations and excitements of motor racing and bullfighting, but also to the sophistication of Beethoven and Tchaikovsky, philosophical conversation and candlelit dinners. 'Jimmy was usually happiest stretched out on my library floor. He loved good music playing in the background.' The Rev James De Weerd was a wounded and decorated hero from the Italian campaign of the Second World War – one of the very few Fairmount residents who had actually seen something substantial of the outside world. His Purple Heart and Silver Star gave him great kudos and popularity among the Fairmount boys, and he used to take some of them to the motor racing in Indianapolis and show them pictures and home movies of the bullfighting he had seen in Mexico. He even encouraged them to build their own rough racing circuit in the field by Marvin Carter's cycle shop, just down the road from the Winslow farm.

That he also took the young boys naked bathing in a YMCA swimming pool was largely ignored. In that mid-west community he was a respected figure. Some eccentricities were to be tolerated from a veteran of the battle of Monte Cassino, an army chaplain who had won his Silver Star rescuing wounded soldiers under fire. After all, the man had a war wound in his midriff the size of a boy's fist.

Second from left in the school basketball team (above); high school baseball, Jimmy centre of picture (below).

In the Quaker team colours.

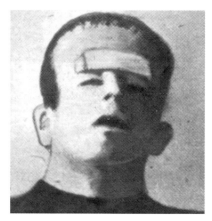

As Frankenstein in 'Goon with the Wind'. .

Self-portrait in clay.

Apart from the introduction to motor racing and bullfighting – beyond acting they were to remain Dean's primary passions – De Weerd was certainly the first person to help the boy towards some understanding and acceptance of his mother's death. He said himself, when Dean was older: 'I taught Jimmy to believe in personal immortality. He had no fear of death because he believed, as I do, that death is merely a control of mind over matter.' Any attitude, or belief, that helped overcome the memory of the physical realities of his mother's death was a liberation for the boy and a curb on the self-pity to which he was prone.

Former *New York Herald Tribune* columnist, Joe Hyams, claimed in his biography, *James Dean: Little Boy Lost*, that De Weerd admitted a sexual relationship with the young James Dean. Certainly the Minister combined father-figure and role model in ways that were both inspirational and seductive, and the young Dean was of an age at which hero-worship and homosexual attraction are a natural part of an adolescent's erotic awakenings. Home in Indiana or in Los Angeles or New York, Dean would always be ready to draw on people who were for him energy forces. Often that energy source became a combination of the cerebral and the sexual. Whether consummated or not, a physical communication with De Weerd might have set that pattern.

This first speculation, claim or rumour sets the pattern for the rest, the truth impossible to evaluate. Paul Alexander (*James Dean, Boulevard of Broken Dreams*) has no doubts that the young Dean lost his virginity to the good-looking, intellectual priest and quotes De Weerd as having said to Hyams: 'Jimmy never mentioned our relationship, nor did I. It would not have helped either of us.'

Other biographers, notably Dalton, Spoto and Holley, have chosen to ignore or deny Hyams's claim. Apart from De Weerd's alleged confession, there is no evidence that he was actively homosexual. Nor were there ever rumours or accusation from any of Fairmount's other young men. But whatever may or not physically have happened between them, De Weerd remains a key figure in Dean's adolescence, widening horizons, showing him history and mankind as epic dramas and helping the young man through some of his turmoil and confusion.

Outside emotional vulnerability there was little to distinguish Dean from any other high-spirited young teenager: the farm boy winning a prize for his stock-raising; the dare-devil, racing motorbikes round Carter's field or 'buzzing' pedestrians up and down Main Street, Fairmount; the schoolboy involving himself successfully in most of the local activities. He was a straight 'A' honour student throughout his high school, a champion pole-vaulter, a hurdler in the track team, a 'sub' in the baseball team, a bespectacled fast guard in basketball. He was also, more significantly, a prize-winner in the art class and President of the Thespian Society.

The violin-playing prodigy had not survived the death of his mother, but the love

Dean on a visit to his old school in February 1955.

for poetry and recitation stayed with him. One day in the classroom a group of boys sniggered while he was reading some verse and Dean had set on them in such a violent fashion that the school authorities were obliged to suspend Dean for the remainder of the week.

Throughout his life Dean was subject to these occasional and usually irrational outbursts of anger and hysteria. The effect of such outbursts was not lost on him and he based a great deal of his early recitation and school acting on similar climaxes of violent histrionics.

His aunt Ortense decided that such passion should be used to better effect, and she brought Jimmy along with her to the local Women's Temperance Union, where he would participate in their drama competitions and even deliver impassioned diatribes against the evils of drinking. He sometimes wrote his own material for these harangues – 'gory odes', he called them – and his tongue-in-cheek fervour actually managed to introduce some humour into their sombre proceedings. 'The way they had it,' Dean would say, 'you could go to hell just for stepping on a grape.'

His talent for debate, recitation and acting was encouraged and coached by the other predominant energy force in his adolescence, Adeline Brookshire Nall, the teacher in charge of drama at the Fairmount High School. Small, dynamic, inspirational and passionate about drama, Adeline recognised very early the raw performing talent of her young student. It was she who persuaded him to enter the annual State Forensic League contest during his senior year at the school. Dean had already distinguished himself that year playing Frankenstein in a high school parody, *Goon With The Wind*. For the contest he chose a recitation in similar vein, an excerpt from Charles Dickens' *Pickwick Papers* entitled

A Madman's Manuscript, a piece which adapted nicely to his shock-tactics style of acting. He came on stage with a blood-curdling scream, ranted and raved his way through the lines, collapsing at the end in spasms of animal frenzy. The judges awarded him the title and entered him for the National contest held later that year in Longmont, Colorado. Dean prepared the same recitation, but ignored Adeline Nall's warning that the piece was too long for the requirements of the National contest. He made a creditable sixth place in the competition, but was bitterly disappointed, and unfairly blamed Adeline Nall for not insisting strongly enough on the cuts she had advised him to make.

Dean's own interior self-expression was perhaps more obvious in his paintings, notwithstanding their derivative style and content. He kept at least two of them in his baggage over the next few years, and they were seen and remembered by some of his friends. One was a caricature of a man as an ashtray, his long arms holding burning cigarettes, his head nothing more than a giant mouth, a hole transfixed with a large cigar. The second, and more sinister painting was entitled 'Man in Woman's Womb' and showed the skeleton of man covered with green skin, standing in sludge oozing from a sewer pipe, one of his arms upraised in fear or pleading, his legs dissolving into the mess around him. It would have been strong material for psychoanalysis, an uncomfortable image from an uneasy mind.

Jimmy Dean graduated from Fairmount High School in the summer of 1949, academically 'above average, good, but handicapped by a lack of application'. He was awarded the school athletics medal and a leaving prize from the art class.

He had arrived in the town nine years previously, lost and very much alone. He had lived the last of his childhood and the greater part of his adolescence in and around this small mid-west farming community, acquiring a second home and family with his uncle, aunt and cousins, and losing some of his loneliness and reticence. He might later write in a poem 'my town hates the Catholic and Jew', but emotionally he would never deny those roots he'd buried in that countryside – even if this middle America, white and protestant, was in no way a worldly preparation for Los Angeles or New York.

He had developed a talent in acting, painting and sport and a strong if still directionless sense of ambition. But apart from his achievements in drama and sport his last year at school and on the farm had, according to his uncle, been restless and undisciplined. He was ready for new stimulus, a vision perhaps of the ideas his mother had dreamed of, a taste of the excitements James De Weerd had described. When his father wrote to him suggesting he start his college education out in California, Jimmy was more than willing to go.

2. Hollywood Student

Our town worships success, the bitch goddess
whose smile hides a taste for blood...
Hedda Hopper

WINTON DEAN had remarried four years after the death of his first wife, retaining his job in Los Angeles, and settling down in another small Santa Monica house. Father and son had seen very little of each other, and Winton Dean was well aware of the emotional crisis his son had suffered following the break-up of the family. Now that Jimmy's schooling was finished Winton was anxious to re-establish a family unit.

One can imagine Dean's apprehension prior to this trip. He was returning to the city where his mother had died, to a father he hardly knew, and to a household presided over by an unknown stepmother. His uncle and aunt, grandparents, and the Rev James De Weerd, all in their different ways helped prepare the boy for the difficulties he would have in adjusting to these situations. As it turned out Jimmy went out of his way to be polite and easy, conforming to his father's wishes even at the sacrifice of his own immediate ambitions.

His father, however, was set against the idea of drama as a suitable university subject. By the end of the summer vacation he had persuaded Jimmy to enrol at the local Santa Monica City College to study pre-law and physical education.

It was to be a year of little achievement for Dean. His father had urged him to take up law, arguing that such a career would make the fullest use of his talent at debate and recitation. Like most parents faced by the wild ambitions of youth, Winton Dean was only anxious to see his son obtain some kind of qualification that would guarantee future employment.

For a time Jimmy was content enough, working his way, not over-energetically, through the general preliminary reading of first year courses and enjoying the new independence of a student's life. He joined as many drama classes as he could find, and in connection with one of them, took a part-time job as a radio announcer on the College FM radio station.

Jean Owen, a drama teacher at Santa Monica, later wrote in *Movieland* about the James Dean she remembered at this time:

> He was always polite and thoughtful; his enthusiasm for everything that pertained to the theatre was boundless... One day in class Jimmy read some scenes from Edgar Allan Poe's *Telltale Heart*. He was magnificent – but then he always had a spectacular emotion for any scene he played. Later, during that same class I asked Jimmy to read

As an outsider in new surroundings, Jimmy experienced the same difficulties as Jim Stark in Rebel.

some scenes from *Hamlet*. That night when I returned home I informed my husband that I had finally found the right student to play Hamlet as I felt it should be played.

A fellow girl student in college, later interviewed for *Picture Post*, has left a more personal image of this 'Hamlet':

> He was shy and awkward, peering through big horn-rimmed glasses at a world that baffled him. One evening a boy I had dated invited him to join our crowd for a beer at 'The Point' – a small café overlooking the Pacific where the younger crowd could go to drink beer, look at the ocean, and talk. But Jimmy wasn't in the talking mood that evening. He contented himself with watching the waves breaking on the shore. He had no use for small-talk.

This brooding young man was an uneasy guest in his father's house. There was never a quarrel, nor even open disagreement; but some time in the new year Dean moved away to share rooms with another student from the City College. By now he had also realised that studies in law and physical education were not going to hold his exclusive interest for much longer. He took steps to enrol at UCLA for the autumn term, planning, as a concession to his father, to transfer the law studies as his major, and take theatre arts as his secondary or minor subject.

During that summer vacation (1950) he took advantage of his PE course, enrolling as an athletics instructor in a local military academy. It was the only time in his life he ever succumbed to a uniform, or to the rigid disciplines of military life. He claimed later to have enjoyed the experience, and professed disappointment when a draft board subsequently turned him down on account of his bad eyesight – though this does not explain his continued appeals against classification up until the time of his death. UN involvement in Korea was looming through these years, the cold war already confrontational after the Berlin airlift. On his 18th birthday Dean was said to have told the draft board back home in Indiana: 'You can't take me, I'm a homosexual.' Given the stigma then attached to homosexuality, it is scarcely credible that the young Dean would have 'come out' so flamboyantly in front of local dignitaries. More probable from his Quaker background is his claim to have been a conscientious objector. The issue of homosexuality was possibly raised in a later written appeal, with or without a psychiatrist's report. Either way, the impatient, ambitious Dean was in no hurry to waste time in uniform.

While working at the military academy Dean had met a second year UCLA student, a member of one of the university sporting fraternities. Even after his twelve months at Santa Monica Dean still felt himself enough of an outsider in the Los Angeles world to jump at the chance of belonging to an exclusive residential fraternity. His job at the academy, and his sporting achievements at the Fairmount High School qualified him for election and that September he became a resident member of the 'Sigma Nu'. As far as his fraternity inmates were concerned he was a pre-law major, and a sporting man. He kept his acting ambitions, and his activities in theatre arts, very much to himself.

Before the term started Dean applied to the Campus Employment Bureau for a part-time job to help with the extra expense of fraternity life. He knew something about cinema projection from one of his classes in Santa Monica, and was given work on the 16mm projectors in the faculties that used visual aid classes. What with his law classes, his job, fraternity life and theatre arts, he would have more activity than he could adequately cope with. But there was now no doubt about his priorities.

At the end of the summer vacation, before starting at UCLA, Dean had used most of his hard-earned salary from the military academy on a trip home to see his relatives and friends. He spent some days helping his uncle with the harvest and, on the afternoon before his journey back to California, rode his motorbike into Marion to see one of the new summer releases – the screen debut of the actor everyone had been talking about in Los Angeles, Marlon Brando. The young tearaway from Broadway theatre was playing

A brief visit home to the farm.

the paraplegic war veteran in Zinnemann's film, *The Men.*

Dean was transfixed. On an unsophisticated, still adolescent level, he quite simply identified with the rebel non-conformist, this handsome young actor-prince from the New York theatre, the slob with his bad language, his blue jeans and his refusal to be overawed or absorbed by the Hollywood system. But more significantly Brando showed Dean a new dimension in acting beyond the skills of recitation or impersonation: namely the exploration of the real life inside a role, and, by implication, the more general search for the truth and understanding of human behaviour. Dean had been overwhelmed by the emotional intensity of Brando's acting. He discovered that Brando's preparation for the role had included four weeks actually living as an inmate in the paraplegic ward of a military hospital. It was a thoroughness and a discipline that appealed to Dean – something beyond the mere titillation of make-believe: something that made acting compatible with a man's own search into the complexities of life and into the confusion of his own emotions.

The articulation of such ideas would come slowly. For the moment all he was sure of was his need for serious acting at whatever level possible. He returned to California that fall of 1950 wholly committed to the ambition of becoming a great actor.

The Theatre Arts faculty at UCLA had considerable advantages over the usual fund-conscious and under-equipped student drama departments. Through carefully fostered relationships with neighbouring Hollywood they had access to the costume and props departments in the major film studios and consequently their productions were as lavishly presented as any expensive Broadway show. Inevitably there was intense competition and in-fighting during the casting of their major productions, and the post-war availability of ex-servicemen in the university made it all the more difficult for younger students to pick up the mature roles. Yet, within a month of enrolling, Dean had already landed himself a good part as Malcolm in *Macbeth*, a production scheduled for that coming December.

Whether he earned this early recognition on his performance in audition, or whether he resorted to faculty politics, no one knows. His good luck certainly surprised, and probably irritated a good many people. Another theatre arts student, William Bast, recalls his first impressions of Dean during this period:

> …the unobtrusive young man with the unruly, sandy-coloured hair, quietly roamed the campus, apparently minding his own business, and only occasionally projecting himself beyond the shell rims of his thick-lensed glasses. He appeared to be nothing more than a simple, withdrawn, little boy, not too long off the farm.

Praised by some, Dean's performance in *Macbeth* was not an unqualified success. The faculty newspaper, *Spotlight*, dismissed him in thirteen unkind words: 'Malcolm failed to show any growth, and would have made a hollow king.' The saving grace for Dean was Malcolm's closing speech, the conclusion of the play, where Malcolm repudiates the Macbeths:

> '- the cruel ministers
> of this dead Butcher and his fiend-like Queen.'

His participation in *Macbeth* had brought him to the unfavourable notice of his hearty brothers at the 'Sigma Nu'. Actors and intellectuals were not encouraged in the fraternity, where competitive sport took precedence over all other activities. On his side Dean was discovering how little he really enjoyed the adolescent rituals of house life. One night at a 'beer-bust', the hearty brethren were taunting him with snide jokes about actors, 'fruits', and ballerinas. They carried their insinuations too far and he lost his temper, laying two of their sporting heroes out on the floor. 'Sigma Nu' solemnly expelled him.

Dean now persuaded his fellow drama student, Bill Bast, to pool resources with him and

James as Malcolm in a UCLA production of Macbeth.

share an apartment. The two of them had become friends more or less accidentally. Their respective girls, Jeanetta and Joanne, were close friends and the four of them had spent the Christmas vacation going round together. Bast and Dean were both 'outsiders' in California, both dedicated hopefuls from the mid-west, and although Bast subsequently turned from acting to writing, the two of them were to remain close friends. Five years later Bast wrote the first authoritative biography following James Dean's death.

That January of 1951 the two of them combed Santa Monica for suitable accommodation, and eventually found a three-room penthouse looking out over tree-tops and the ocean. As an apartment it was far too expensive, but too perfect to turn down. According to Bast it was Jimmy who made the decision by prancing about the rooms, testing all the furniture, the shower, the toilet, the fridge, the oven, every cupboard door and the sun-deck outside. He then sat himself in the middle of the floor and announced his intention of living there. The down-payment for the first month's rent cleaned them both out, and from that day on the struggle for survival was defined in terms of cash and part-time jobs. Bast had found work as a uniformed usher at the CBS building and soon picked up a small part in one of their radio productions. He shared his professional contacts with Dean and they were both included in one of the CBS 'radio workshop' dramas.

It was one of the attractions, and academic disadvantages, of studying drama at UCLA, that the 'big-time' beckoned from so near. Most of the acting members of theatre arts spent a good deal of time canvassing for work down the road in the film, television, and radio studios.

Another UCLA Theatre Arts student, James Bellah, was Dean's stepping-stone to his first film performance. Son of the novelist, James Warner Bellah, he had better access than most of the students to the world of showbiz and had acquired an agent, Isabel Draesemer. Through her, Bellah was asked to gather a group of young-looking 18-year-olds for a two minute Pepsi-Cola commercial (shooting with under-18s, the production company would have been bound by the limited hours of work enforced for juveniles). They were hired as Non-Guild amateurs on a straight ten dollar a day fee. The first day's sequence was filmed on a merry-go-round in Griffith Park (the location later used for the planetarium scenes in *Rebel Without a Cause*). The best of the first day's participants were then chosen for the second day of interior work, among them James Dean, and an actor and actress who were to appear with him in *Rebel*, four years later – Nick Adams and Beverley Long.

The director had picked out Dean as the central figure in the commercial, and, as a result, Isabel Draesemer took Dean on as one of her clients. The Pepsi-Cola commercial had also given the young actors the opportunity to acquire the elusive union card. It seemed at the time a major breakthrough for Dean, and it certainly hastened the end of his connections with the Theatre Arts department at UCLA. He had made no progress there since his comparative failure in *Macbeth*, and when they passed him over for their forthcoming spring production, *Dark of the Moon*, his disappointment turned to angry disdain. He took no further part in any of their official activities.

Besides his own personal disillusion, Dean now had good reason to concentrate his acting studies outside the faculty classes. Bill Bast had organised nine of the more dedicated theatre arts students, including Dean, into an acting study group under the informal guidance of James Whitmore, a professional actor and acquaintance of Bast. Whitmore had been a student at the Actors Wing and a member of the Actors Studio in New York, where he had been coached by Lee Strasberg and Elia Kazan. He had played in the Broadway production of *Command Decision*, and had been nominated that very year for an Academy Award as Best Supporting Actor for his performance as Kinnie in William

Wellman's *Battleground.* An experienced and dedicated actor, sympathetic to their ambitions, he was the ideal guide to introduce the young students to the principles of the so-called Stanislavsky 'method'.

These informal classes, held in an empty room over the Brentwood Country Mart, were crucial to the development of Dean's acting. Conversant only with the mechanics and effects of declamatory extrovert acting, he had never examined the psychological processes of interior acting, the absorption of actor into his role, the transformations made possible through concentration. He began now to understand the inner conviction necessary to the intensity of acting he had so admired in Brando's screen performance.

The early exercises in Whitmore's classes consisted of no more than basic movements and mimes, during which the actor had to retain the interest of the other eight students by communicating tension or mystery through his own efforts of concentration, without using words or sounds.

The next stage in Whitmore's tuition was to set up hypothetical situations between two actors and let them loose to improvise a scene. Bill Bast and James Dean did one such scene together: a jeweller (Bast) trying to detain a thief (Dean) long enough for the police to arrive; the thief instead trying to reclaim a stolen watch he has left with the jeweller for repair. After several unconvincing attempts at the scene, Whitmore told Dean to sit apart for a while, until he felt he had acquired the whole reality of that thief, his fear and his urgency. When Dean was ready they started the scene again and this time he had absorbed himself so completely into the role that both actors finally lost control of the scene. Even Dean's appearance seemed to have changed as he became that thief, frightened and savage, abusing Bill Bast's shopkeeper so effectively that Bast lost his temper. Before they reached the end of the scene the two of them were fighting in earnest and Whitmore had to pull them apart: 'Jimmy remained at a high level of nervous excitement for a while, but soon after the meeting broke up he slipped into a state of depression. The experience, although revealing and rewarding, had been physically and mentally exhausting.'

This 'hangover' effect, unwinding after the emotional tension of any intense piece of interior acting, would remain a problem for Dean throughout his acting career. In these group sessions Whitmore was more concerned with the preparation leading up to a piece of acting and was content to limit analysis and criticism afterwards to a bare minimum. Later, as a member of the New York Actors Studio or as a professional in the theatre or on television and film sets, Dean would find there was little time for 'unwinding', and consequently he had a low emotional tolerance of criticism, however valid and constructive.

Dean soon had his first opportunity to put these new skills into practice. The producer of the Pepsi-Cola commercial, Jerry Fairbanks, was putting together a lavish TV production for that Easter, *Hill Number One.* Reminded by Draesemer of his Pepsi-Cola star, Fairbanks cast Dean as John the Baptist.

The play was a parallel narrative, cutting between the efforts of a platoon of soldiers trying to capture a hill (probably Korea) and the events following Christ's crucifixion in Jerusalem. John the Baptist made peripheral appearances with only a handful of lines in the whole play. Even so Dean was apparently in an agony of nerves throughout rehearsals and shooting. Apart from the Pepsi-Cola commercial – little more than a montage of faces and reactions – he had never seen himself on film, and had never appreciated the need to restrain gestures and facial movements for the screen. He told Nick Adams at the time: 'I build up this head of steam like in Jimmy Whitmore's exercises, but where in class you then let it rip, on film you've got to keep it all bottled up. It makes me look like my bladder's bursting.'

As St John in 'Hill Number One'.

Dean's part in the play was small and, in the company of professionals, his acting was apparently not very impressive. Yet his screen presence made an immediate impact on at least one section of the Los Angeles audience, precursors of the legend. The girls of the Immaculate Heart High School had been told to watch the film during their Easter vacation, and a few days later they contacted Dean through his agent, inviting him to a tea-party to inaugurate the 'Immaculate Heart James Dean Appreciation Society'. All praise to the girls for anticipating events by some four years! Dean submitted, uncomplaining, to a succession of lemonade parties and giggling flattery and apparently made the most of his sudden and temporary stardom with these pretty teenagers.

This early fan club was the only tangible result from *Hill Number One*, and the only uplift in an otherwise depressing summer. Dean had waited expectantly, but in vain, for offers of work to follow his performance. Before very long the film was forgotten, Dean's money had run out, and he was back once more a penniless student, though by now entirely divorced from his studies at UCLA. He had believed himself on the edge of the big time and became instead just one more of the legion of hopefuls haunting the Burbank bars and offices. His flatmate, Bill Bast, watched him with some concern:

> Jimmy became subject to more frequent periods of depression and would slip off into a silent mood at least once each day… If I had thought it difficult to communicate with him at other times in the past, I had never known such lack of communication as existed during his fits of depression… He would sit in his room, sit there and stare into space for hours. I made several attempts to get through to him, but rarely got more than a grunt or a distant stare for a response.

They were both in the same financial predicament and both tired of chasing rainbows round the casting offices. But, while Bast was keeping up his UCLA studies, Dean had now dropped out of classes altogether. His whole way of life at this time was full of uncertainty and lack of purpose. At his worst he was thought to have joined the street-corner hustlers, the would-be stars who believed that magic doors could be opened on a midnight pick-up with an ageing actress or a homosexual producer. Did Dean share the futility of their tired fantasies, borrow their old jokes and join them in their grim midnight assignations? Three years later Dean is alleged to have told his friend Jonathan Gilmore that during those earlier months as a student and hopeful in Los Angeles he'd 'had his cock sucked by five of the biggest names in Hollywood' – the dishonourable tradition of the casting couch that, as ever in history, abuses but rarely delivers. In retrospect, and if true, it seemed almost to amuse Dean. Sex or no sex, results or no results, these had been inelegant adventures.

The only antidote to whatever increasing sense of self-disgust was the mood of serious dedication in the periodic meetings of Whitmore's study group. Dean later paid tribute to the help and advice he received from Whitmore at this time: 'I owe a lot to him. I guess you can say he saved me when I got all mixed up. He told me I didn't know the difference between acting as a soft job and acting as a difficult art. I needed to learn these differences.'

More practical help came from his room-mate. Bast was still working part-time as an usher at CBS and, when Dean had spent his modest earnings from *Hill Number One*, Bast persuaded his boss to take his room-mate on in a similar capacity. Dean lasted only one short week, ridiculing his uniform, the 'monkey-suit' he called it, and refusing to adopt the obsequious tones and gestures the job demanded. It was the start, however short-lived and small-scale, of his running battle with establishment attitudes in Hollywood.

By now Bast was supporting Dean on his part-time salary, even paying for the petrol to run Dean's old jalopy – a '39 Chevrolet, bought by Winton Dean for his son's twentieth birthday. Relations between the two flatmates, already strained, became finally impossible when they both fell for the same girl.

Bast was courting a young actress he had met at CBS, Beverly Wills, daughter of the comedienne Joan Davis. Although Beverly was already playing in a weekly radio comedy, *Junior Miss*, she was still in high school and when her class held their summer picnic Bast invited Dean to join their party – an occasion which Beverly recalled for *Modern Screen* some six years later:

> I thought he was pretty much of a creep until we got to the picnic and then all of a sudden he came to life. We began to talk about acting and Jimmy lit up. He told me how interested he was in the Stanislavsky method, where you not only act people, but things too.
>
> 'Look,' said Jimmy, 'I'm a pine tree in a storm.' He held his arms out and waved wildly. To feel more free, he impatiently tossed off his cheap, tight, blue jacket. He looked bigger as soon as he did, because you could see his broad shoulders and powerful build. Then he got wilder and pretended he was a monkey. He climbed a big tree and swung from a high branch. Dropping from the branch he landed on his hands like a little boy, chuckling uproariously at every little thing. Once in the spotlight, he ate it up and had us all in stitches all afternoon. The 'creep' had turned into the hit of the party.

From then on Dean used to double-date with Bill and Beverly, pairing off either with one of Beverly's girlfriends or with Jeanetta Lewis from the Theatre Arts department at UCLA. Often these double-dates would end up at Joan Davis' luxurious Bel-Air home, where food and drink were plentiful and generously available to the two starving young students. Bill was usually occupied in his usher's job at CBS and it was Dean who took over the chore of meeting Beverly from work and from school. The two of them started to spend time together, playing golf and learning archery, and after a few weeks Beverly decided she preferred Jimmy to Bill. Bill Bast was undiplomatic enough to complain to Jeanetta Lewis about this misfortune, only to find out from the enraged Jeanetta that Jimmy was also still dating her. Jeanetta persuaded Bast it was time to move out of the penthouse and leave Dean to fend for himself. There was an angry, and, in the end, violent scene between the three of them with Jimmy lashing out at Jeanetta for breaking up the friendship.

The friendship with Bill Bast had been the only lasting relationship of any depth in two years of his Los Angeles life. But in some way the friendship had been a cushion for Dean against realities he had not wished to face. Bast was the more mature of the two, the more sophisticated, the more practical: the one to keep careful hold of his part-time job at CBS; the one to have continued his studies at UCLA; and, when times were hard, the one who had to go out and borrow money from friends. Dean now had to pick himself up and start coping on his own. He had not only lost his room-mate, but also the wherewithal to pay the rent; and to this extent the temporary bust-up between the two friends was probably beneficial.

Appropriately enough it was Beverly who came to his rescue, lending him the next month's rent, while he began to re-establish old contacts in his search for employment.

Isabel Draesemer had found him no work since the Easter play and Dean gravitated back to CBS. One of the ushers with whom he had worked during that brief week in the 'monkey-suit' – Ted Avery – had since transferred to work in the adjoining car park. He now fixed Dean a job as part-time attendant, and introduced him to the regular clients, producers and actors working at CBS.

Ted Avery was also picking up the occasional bit-parts in Westerns and he began teaching Dean some of his trick-riding and roping. The two of them were often to be seen, and heard, dressed up and acting as cow-pokes, whooping along the CBS corridors. When Avery's wife left town on holiday, Dean moved into their small Hollywood flat. It was Ted Avery who now gave him the introductions that led to his first work in major feature films. They were moving in the sub-strata of the Hollywood power structure, the assistant directors and associate producers, distributing their patronage and favours with one-day engagements in one-line bit parts. It had little to do with acting ability and offered still less in the way of prestige or recognition. But it was paid work, and, on a limited scale, a means of gaining experience on major feature film units.

Dean worked on three pictures during the next few weeks: as a soldier in the Twentieth Century production, *Fixed Bayonets* (his one line – 'It's a rear guard coming back'); as a silent, sour-looking sailor in a Dean Martin/Jerry Lewis comedy for Paramount, *Sailor Beware*; and finally as an ice-cream 'gourmet' in a Universal-International picture with Rock Hudson, Charles Coburn, and Piper Laurie, *Has Anybody Seen My Gal?* (his one long line delivered to Charles Coburn – 'Hey Gramps, I'll have a choc malt, heavy on the choc, plenty of milk, four spoons of malt, two scoops of vanilla ice cream, one mixed with the rest, and one floating').

With so much new incident in his life it was not long before Dean searched out Bill Bast to share some of the excitement. Their quarrel was forgotten and Bast was given a first hand account of the finale to his friend's short-lived romance with Beverly Wills. After disagreement with her mother he took to meeting Beverly in the dance pavilion at Paradise Cove. Jimmy was no great dancer. Beverly was not only good but insatiable. One evening after watching her pirouette for hours on end with a succession of young men, he lost patience: 'Dance your fool head off,' he shouted at her and walked out.

According to Beverly the disagreement had built up over a longer period, and was symptomatic of Jimmy's emotional insecurity at the time. The other boys at Paradise Cove tended to exclude him or look down on him and he in return was quick to take offence. As with Jeanetta, his break-up with Beverly ended with a violent scene, on this occasion a fight with one of Beverly's dancing partners.

Apart from his work in bit-parts, Dean was soon to find further work on radio shows. Parking cars one day at the CBS lot, he met Rogers Brackett, a young, articulate, radio and commercials director and one of the minority of genuinely cultured intellectuals in Hollywood. Aside from helping him obtain small radio parts (*Alias Jane Doe* and *Stars Over Hollywood*), Brackett acted as a stimulant on Dean's innate, but by now almost dormant, intellectual appetite, introducing him to the worlds of Cocteau and Colette. He taught Dean the importance of understanding the historical and cultural context of writers and artists. Bill Bast remembers the effect of this education: 'Most of his newly found sophistication was becoming to him. Although a worldly way of thinking was completely new to him, he took it in his stride, even appearing blasé and unimpressed with all he was learning and all he was experiencing. Rogers had taught him not only to participate in a society of sophisticates, but also to remain intellectually aloof and objective…' The natural successor to James De Weerd.

Of all Dean's supposed or claimed homosexual relationships, this friendship with Rogers Brackett is the most documented and the most authentic. Before his death in 1979, Brackett granted Ronald Martinetti (*The James Dean Story*) an interview 'to set the record straight'. His own recollections suggested a genuinely reciprocal relationship, mentor-protegé, father and son. He did comment: 'If it was a father-son relationship, it was also somewhat incestuous,' though Brackett insisted that the sexual content of their friendship was not one-sided but a mutual physical enjoyment.

When Ted Avery's wife returned to Hollywood Dean had to vacate their tiny flat and Brackett offered him accommodation in his Sunset Plaza apartment. The move brought Dean into close contact with the swimming pool and cocktails circuit. For a few weeks he shared some of the superficial glamour and glitter of the 'Strip' set, becoming addicted with the rest of them to the spurious thrills of dropping names and passing gossip. Being a natural clown and impersonator, he was a popular enough guest at parties, or on the weekend trips to see the bullfights across the Mexican border in Tijuana.

What further sexual involvement, if any, he had with Brackett's gay friends and their acquaintances is impossible to know but it did not take long for the novelty and excitement to wear thin. Dean had no illusions about his role in this social whirl, though his comment was perhaps less than fair to Brackett himself. 'What a pile of hog-wash,' he told Bill Bast. 'With all their power and wealth they've got it in their heads that they're gods. This town's full of them. They get these poor kids, saps like me, and make them perform. You know – run around like court-jesters charming the pants off important people… I thought it might pay off. But it doesn't take long to find out it won't. I'm not performing for any of them. Not any more. And if I can't make it on my talent, I don't want to make it at all.'

On one level Dean was reacting against what he felt as a loss of self-respect: he could see little difference between the pool-side big-shots and the midnight hustlers he had associated with earlier in the summer. On the practical level he was beginning to realise that the majority of bit-part actors would spend the rest of their acting lives on the same head-busting hustle and in the same one-day, one-line engagements.

Both Whitmore and Brackett had recognised Dean's potential talent. Now they were both telling him to get himself out of Hollywood before he made roots. Go east, they told him; where the theatre lives; where Strasberg and Kazan teach; where an actor can train. Go to New York.

But there was something almost cosy about Los Angeles, even when the jobs were hard to find. One could pretend to be still a student; and there were friends of a sort, to whom he could turn: his father down the road in Santa Monica; James Whitmore for advice and coaching; Bill Bast and the students at UCLA; the hustlers and the hopefuls in the bars and on the beaches. Perhaps Rogers Brackett's own move out of Los Angeles to work in Chicago swayed the decision for him.

When he did leave it was a spontaneous move that left no time for second thoughts. Bill Bast returned one night to his apartment-hotel and found a telephone message under the door: 'Mr Dean called. Gone to New York.'

3. New York Apprentice

What is essential is invisible to the eye...
The Little Prince

J AMES DEAN stopped twice on his way across the continent: in Chicago to stay some days with Rogers Brackett; and in Fairmount to visit his family and friends. Brackett took him to some shows and gave him introductions; his uncle and aunt concealed their misgivings, and the Rev De Weerd lent him two hundred dollars. Thus equipped and encouraged the twenty-year-old James Dean arrived for the first time in his life on Manhattan Island; and all but turned tail and ran.

'New York overwhelmed me. For the first few weeks I only strayed a couple of blocks from my hotel off Times Square. I would see three movies a day in an attempt to escape from my loneliness and depression. I spent a hundred and fifty dollars of my limited funds just on seeing movies.'

It was a new dimension of loneliness for Dean. After his mother's death he had known aloneness in the company of others, on the farm with his uncle and aunt, at school, in college, or sharing with room-mates. But he had never experienced such complete physical isolation. The initial effect on him seems to have been debilitating and demoralising, and it was some time before he found the energy or courage to use the professional introductions Brackett had given him. Only when his money had run out and he was forced to take part-time jobs, did he begin to make real contact with the city, working as busboy or counterman in the drugstores and restaurants of midtown Manhattan.

Dean's personal introduction to the New York scene had come through Brackett's friend, the composer Alec Wilder, then a resident at the legendary Algonquin Hotel on West 44th Street, with its 'round table' of artists and intellectuals. Wilder suggested the nearby and more modest Iroquois Hotel for Dean – where he lived until money ran low and he moved to the YMCA on West 63rd.

The first of Brackett's professional introductions took Dean to a New York television director, James Sheldon, working at that time on the *Robert Montgomery Presents* show. After inevitable delays and postponements Sheldon gave Dean an audition, and though there were no suitable parts available in his own show, he was impressed enough with the young actor to recommend him to the Louis Schurr Agency. A few days later when Dean called in for his appointment at the Schurr office no one seemed particularly anxious to see him. He was eventually interviewed by Schurr's assistant, Jane Deacy. Against the advice of others in the office, she agreed to take him on as a client. Her obstinacy was a major turning point for Dean. He had found one of the rare guardian angels of showbiz: an agent prepared to work hard for an unknown, unrecognised, and unrealised talent.

Little precise detail is known about Jane Deacy's influence on James Dean. After his death she steadfastly refused to give interviews or information of any sort. But she was certainly the guiding hand behind his television and film career, vetting his offers, and at times holding him back to wait for the right kind of part and the best opportunity. On his side Dean seems to have accepted her advice and decisions without argument, and up to the very day of his death it was 'Mom' Deacy who was still organising his timetable of work and the strategy of his career and contracts.

There were many times during those early months in New York when Dean would lose patience with the endless auditions and the slow progress he was making. She told him clearly: 'You're every bit as good as you think you are. But it's going to be a long time and hard work making other people understand that.'

Whether through Jane Deacy or James Sheldon, Dean's first job was as 'off-stage' stooge on the *Beat the Clock* television show – a regular competition comedy programme in which competitors had to carry out bizarre gags or stunts in front of a live audience (similar to the later BBC and Eurovision shows *It's a Knockout* and *Jeux sans Frontières*, where competitors were instead grouped in teams). The main attraction of the programme was simply to watch the participants making fools of themselves. However, the rules of the show stipulated that all the gags and stunts should be physically possible and James Dean was one of the actors employed to test each stunt before the programmes. His natural aptitude for clowning overcame any hesitations he might have felt about standing as a dumb target for buckets of water and custard pies, and he would work for hours at the more difficult stunts to prove them possible.

Occasionally the participants were allowed to see the actors performing some of the more intricate exercises and rehearse their own attempts. The producers found Dean particularly adept at relaxing nervous debutantes, and he was eventually 'promoted' to the pre-broadcast audience-warming sessions. But in the end his own physical prowess lost him the job. He was too good at the stunts and made them look altogether too easy.

Dean was still living in one-room claustrophobia at a modest YMCA hostel and slowly enlarging his circle of New York acquaintances. While in Chicago with Rogers Brackett he had met a television script writer, David Swift, and the actress, Maggie McNamara. They were now both back in town, and with them and their friends, and in particular with the lyricist Bill Envig and the composer Alec Wilder, Dean was finding the intellectual ambience and stimulus he always craved. Like De Weerd, Whitmore and Brackett before, they took on the role of his 'teachers', and with them he overcame the solitude and depression of those earlier New York weeks.

His life was built round casting sessions, and the interminable waiting for offers of work that were slow to materialise. During that winter, 1951–52, he starred in a radio 'Theatre Guild of the Air' and picked up bit-parts in at least five of the TV drama series: *Treasury-Men in Action*, *Tales of Tomorrow*, *Martin Kane*, *Kraft Theatre*, and *Danger*. There are no records or details of the parts he played in these melodramas and one can only assume they were too small to attract attention at the time, or to be remembered later. The work itself was probably more demanding of his tolerance than of his skills. These were the early boom years of television drama, when the networks were expanding too fast for the studios. The sheer volume of work being turned out, most of it 'live', meant there was little time to perfect scripts or performances.

Dean, a bit-part performer, still a mere face in the crowd, watched these productions with growing disenchantment, and the reputation he acquired as a troublesome actor seems to date from his first year in the New York studios. It is difficult to know how far his bad

New York.

reputation was justified, and how much of it was accumulated and exaggerated in later legend. It seems that directors and producers lost patience with his time-wasting demands as he tried to find dimensions in what were little more than walk-on parts. They were only interested in a slick professional interpretation that did not create complications in the short periods of rehearsal at their disposal. Nor were they accustomed to Dean's extraordinary informality of dress and manner. The image of an actor in the early fifties was still associated with the well-cut sports jacket, well-pressed trousers and well-groomed smile. Dean would cause minor – and calculated? – sensations when he turned up to rehearsals, scruffy, scowling and unshaven in his raincoat, dirty blue jeans and T-shirt; and even once when his shoes had been soaked in a downpour, barefoot.

There is nothing more than hearsay evidence or statistics to judge the extent of his reputed bad behaviour, and insofar as they are complete, the statistics show that after this early flurry of bit-parts, Dean had a long period of inactivity (during the summer of 1952), possibly as a result of his difficult reputation.

Sometime during that first winter Dean had left his one-room prison at the YMCA, and moved into an apartment on Seventy-second Street which he shared with a young dancing student, Elizabeth ('Dizzy') Sheridan, daughter of the pianist Frank Sheridan. They had met as two lonely and insolvent outsiders at one of the New York acting clubs or bars and, pooling resources, kept each other company through most of the winter. Dizzy was working as a part-time usherette at the Paris Cinema near the Hotel Plaza. According to people who knew her at the time, she was an attractive, friendly girl, unpretentious and very broke. Theirs was to be a very close, intimate, mutually supportive love affair that would continue to wind its way in and out of Dean's life until the final months of his work in Hollywood.

Eventually they had to leave Seventy-second Street, apparently for lack of funds. Rogers Brackett had arrived in New York from Chicago and Dean moved into the West Twenties to share an attic flat with him – while continuing to see Dizzy in her temporary one-room lodging on Eighth Avenue. It was the only period in which his heterosexual life came into direct confrontation or competition with the life and, if it still existed on Dean's side, the love he and Rogers Brackett shared. There was an understandable coolness between Dizzy and Rogers, with Dean apparently encouraging the girl to stand up to his mentor.

Neither Brackett, nor Bast, nor Dizzy Sheridan ever mentioned the wilder homosexual adventures Dean is alleged to have pursued in New York with what Paul Alexander calls 'the fist-fuck set'. In *Boulevard of Broken Dreams* he claims a highly promiscuous, uninhibited, even sado-masochistic side to Dean's early New York life – stand-up arse-fucking in the open doorway of a young male dancer's apartment, a kneel-down blow job in a crowded party, 'human ashtray' S&M, a willingness to experiment with any sort of sexual activity. Such claims read more like fantasies and have never been substantiated.

The West Twenties did not last long. For whatever reason, living-in with Rogers Brackett was not an arrangement that Dean much enjoyed and when his old Santa Monica room-mate Bill Bast migrated out from Los Angeles, Dean decided to share a room with him back at the Iroquois Hotel. Though he continued to sponsor his young friend, Rogers believed he had now lost Dean's affection to Bill Bast, though there is no indication from Dean, from Bast himself or from any of their friends that theirs was ever a sexual relationship, either earlier in Los Angeles or now in New York.

Bast had come east looking for writing work, disillusioned and depressed by Hollywood, uncertain of his own future. He expected to find Dean in much the same state of mind and was surprised instead by his friend's apparent serenity in the face of continuing hardship and disappointment. The roles in their relationship had been

strangely reversed: 'No longer was I the one with my feet planted firmly on the ground…
No longer was it Jimmy who turned to me for the answers, as it had been in the beginning.
Now I was following Jimmy's lead…'

Dean told him he had discovered his new attitude or philosophy in Antoine de Saint
Exupery's fairy-tale *The Little Prince,* the story of a child from a distant planet who
embodies love, kindness, friendship, simplicity and understanding: 'the little man who
laughs, who has golden hair, and refuses to answer questions'.

Rogers Brackett had introduced Dean to the book, and now Dean passed his copy on to
Bill Bast. The philosophy of *The Little Prince* became a motto for the two friends: 'What is
essential is invisible to the eye.'

Jane Deacy had been trying to encourage Dean's original ambition to join the Actors
Studio, but there was a strong reluctance on his part to submit himself to the ordeal of their
audition, the ultimate test for any aspiring young actor. The failure rate at the Studio was
very high and Dean was wary of risking his fragile confidence.

One day in the spring or early summer of 1952 he met a young actress in the Schurr
office and discovered she was writing an audition scene to present at the Studio.

'I was typing in the office and this funny little boy with glasses on was leaning on a
door-frame. He was really annoying me because I wanted to get on with what I was doing.
He came and looked over my shoulder, and asked what it was, and I said, "I'm writing a
play." And he said, "Can I read a scene?" Which I didn't want him to do, so he got hostile.
I asked him whether he was an actor. He said, "I hope so," and I said, "Well you don't look
like one." At which point he went out and left me alone.

'When I left later he was sitting out in the lobby. So I walked over and said, "I didn't
mean to be rude. My name is Christine White." And he looked up and said, "My name's
Jim. Would you like to have a cup of coffee?"

'He couldn't stop talking, and we went downstairs and had coffee. When he took off
his glasses he wasn't too bad-looking. Very underweight. And wearing a borrowed
sweater.'

Christine White was also a client of Jane Deacy and it is possible that this meeting was
deliberately arranged by Miss Deacy, for it proved to be the encouragement or stimulus
that Dean needed. He offered to help Chris White work on her play, and as they discussed
it together it developed into a sketch involving both of them: a brief encounter between a
boy and girl on a deserted beach, evoking a mood of fear and despair.

The scene was revised many times, tried out variously on friends, in bars, on street-
corners, until it had achieved a strong enough realism to provoke reaction and even
participation from unsuspecting onlookers. But on the day of the audition Dean was still
so apprehensive of the Studio that he tried to postpone the examination, insisting that
they were not adequately prepared. Fortunately Chris White was made of sterner stuff,
and would not let him back out. At her insistence and with the help of two quick beers,
Dean stumbled short-sightedly on stage in front of the evangelists of American acting,
Lee and Molly Strasberg, and theatre and movie director, Elia Kazan. Chris White
remembers: 'Jimmy was as blind as a bat without his glasses, but he wouldn't wear them
when he was acting. In our scene he was supposed to be in the middle of the stage and I
was supposed to come in and trip over him. He couldn't find the middle and he went all
the way to the end. If I'd have tripped over him I'd have been off-stage, so we had to
improvise.'

Instead of appearing on stage and falling over him, Chris White sat herself down
centre stage and left it to Dean to make the necessary adjustment: 'The surprise start
created a good tension. It was unsettling and we were both like fire-crackers from then on.'

James Dean and Chris White were both chosen from the one hundred and fifty applicants. Lee Strasberg later recalled that, 'Dean made an excellent impression at the audition. He never again performed as well for us as at that audition.'

At twenty-one Dean was reputedly the youngest member of the Studio and he wrote a hopeful letter home to his uncle and aunt in Fairmount:

> I have made great strides in my craft. After months of auditioning I am very proud to announce that I am a member of the Actors Studio. The greatest school of the theatre. It houses great people like Marlon Brando, Julie Harris, Arthur Kennedy, Elia Kazan, Mildred Dunnock, Kevin McCarthy, Monty Clift, June Havoc, and on and on and on. Very few get into it, and it is absolutely free. It is the best thing that can happen to an actor. I am one of the youngest to belong. ...If I can keep this up and nothing interferes with my progress, one of these days I might be able to contribute something to the world...

The Actors Studio had been established in 1947 by Elia Kazan and Cheryl Crawford as an attempt to recreate the opportunities of training and experiment that had characterised the Group Theatre of the 1930s. The Russian teachers, Boleslavsky and Ouspenskaya, had introduced Stanislavsky's principles of an actor's training and preparation into America in the mid-1920s, and the Group Theatre had developed as a repertory of this new naturalism, involving writers and directors as well as actors (the Strasbergs, Harold Clurman, Cheryl Crawford, Clifford Odets, Kazan, John Garfield, Franchot Tone). Elia Kazan was the major link between the fringe theatres of the 1930s and a new realism in acting and stage production on Broadway: '...the whole idea of the Group Theatre was to get poetry out of the common things of life. That was fired up by the Depression and our reaction to it. We felt that the whole basis of society had to be changed. Then there was another element: the Stanislavsky system made us see more in the lives of human beings and it became our mission to reveal greater depths. Also, at that time, Freud had become popularised. All these trends came together in the Group Theatre: the political left, the introduction to Freud and Marx, the absolute, idealistic dedication and determination towards a new world.'

By 1940 the Group Theatre had faded away with nothing to replace its function as a drama nursery, and when Kazan became established as Broadway's leading director after the war, he set up the Actors Studio to fill this void. In its early years teaching had been taken on by Kazan and Robert Lewis, but by the time James Dean arrived in New York the Studio was being run by the Strasbergs. Because of his film and theatre commitments, Kazan was only intermittently involved in auditions or coaching.

Dean certainly felt, at the time and afterwards, that his association with the Actors Studio was an important event in his life. But it is less certain how much the Studio contributed directly to his acting.

We cannot even be sure for how long or how often Dean attended classes. In the aftermath of his death, when 'method actors' were in general opprobrium, Kazan was trying to repudiate the 'mumble-scratch' image with which the Studio acting had been labelled and he seemed to suggest that Dean's connection with the Studio had been tenuous: 'Everyone got the idea that it was a sloppily dressed, don't-give-a-damn kind of group. This is not so. To begin with Dean was scarcely at the Studio at all. He came in a few times and slouched in a front row. He never participated in anything.'

Lee Strasberg instead remembers Dean being more closely involved with the classes, and feels that Dean's irregular attendance was due to the practical difficulties of having to take work in order to pay for food and lodging.

The relationship between Dean and the Actors Studio remains thus ambiguous. When Strasberg later opened an Actors Studio in Hollywood, a James Dean poster was a required part of the decor and, along with Marilyn Monroe, Marlon Brando and Montgomery Clift, his is the name most immediately connected with the school. Yet it seems all three of them did very little actual studying or training at the Studio. Once they had acquired the Stanislavsky philosophy, they possessed the natural talent to develop on their own.

The simplest definition of this 'philosophy' is that the actor should not 'imitate' or 'impersonate' but that he should 'become' the part by working out a link between the role and the reality of his own life and emotions. In practice this meant learning how to develop complete self-awareness, both physically and mentally.

Dean was already conversant with most of the training techniques and exercises employed at the Studio, having practised them in James Whitmore's classes back in Los Angeles. The one new element Dean had not yet experienced was the concentration of criticism and analysis as applied by Lee Strasberg.

Strasberg is familiar to more recent audiences for his role in *The Godfather Part II* as the dying but still ruthless underworld boss, Hyman Roth, a performance for which he received

Lee Strasberg in action.

an Oscar nomination. It was a part well suited to him. Small in stature, untidy in appearance and apparently unprepossessing, Strasberg in his time had crucified many of the great names: Marlon Brando, Rod Steiger, Eli Wallach, Geraldine Page, Shelley Winters, Tony Franciosa, Paul Newman; they were all, even in their later success, fearful of performing in front of him. In his book *Marilyn*, Norman Mailer describes Strasberg in action:

> He would watch a performance at the Studio without a quiver of emotion and then, in the silence that followed the discussion of the actors and the class, he would begin (with an air of annoyance at the simplicity of other opinions) to speak. He could talk for fifteen minutes on a scene that had taken five, he could go on for half an hour if the subject was worthy of analysis. He had one illimitable subject to which he always returned – it was the elusive question of how an actor might find a route from his own personality to the part he should play, and, it was probably inconceivable to Strasberg that this process could be faultless. He would see flaws in the most superb performance. Chief engineer of spiritual mechanics, he was able to trace a performance's inability to deliver an absolute maximum of emotion at climax to that faintest slip of concentration which had occurred picking up a pack of cigarettes some minutes earlier…

Such analysis was invaluable to the class that had watched the performance, but was valuable to the performers themselves only in so far as they could withstand such a psychological onslaught. The first time Dean was faced with this treatment from Lee Strasberg he was reciting and acting the monologue of a matador preparing for his last bullfight. Given his own obsessive knowledge and love of the *corrida* this was subject matter ripe for Dean's over-indulgence, and Strasberg laid into him. Dean slung his matador's cape over one shoulder and walked out of the class, apparently never again to participate in readings or performances. No one can remember for certain when this 'walk-out' took place – certainly sometime during that summer or autumn of 1952.

Dean explained his reaction afterwards to Bill Bast: 'I don't know what's inside of me. I don't know what happens when I act… But if I let them dissect me, like a rabbit in a clinical research laboratory or something, I might not be able to produce again. They might sterilise me. That man had no right to tear me down like that. You keep knocking a guy down and you take the guts away from him. And what's an actor without guts?'

The reaction was true to character: not merely the bewilderment Dean so often experienced in the face of criticism, but a deep-felt aversion to anything that might expose or explain the inner emotions from which he lived and acted. A similar repugnance or fear was to drive him from a psychiatrist's consulting-room three years later. It was the one obscurity in his world he would rather leave unexamined, unexplained: that darkness in himself. He knew how to draw on it for his acting and that for the moment was enough. The spirit existed, good or evil, and he had no wish to exorcise it.

Dean's early weeks of attendance or non-attendance at the Actors Studio coincided with a lean period in his television work. He and Bill Bast (now working temporarily in publicity) were forced to give up their room at the Iroquis and share a summer let with an ex-UCLA Theatre Arts girl they had known back in Los Angeles. The three of them were caretaking an apartment on Forty-sixth Street while the owners were away.

Dean had to take odd jobs, working first as an ice-heaver on a refrigerator truck, then on a tug-boat on the Hudson River. The little experience he picked up as a deck-hand was put to good use later in the summer, when he was invited to join the crew on a yacht belonging to the Broadway producer, Lemuel Ayers.

Ayers was another friend of Rogers Brackett whose network of (mostly gay) contacts continued to prove useful to Dean. When Brackett visited New York in the early summer he had taken Dean out for a weekend at the Ayers' riverside home. Dean was well aware that Ayers was planning to put N. Richard Nash's play *See the Jaguar* onto Broadway later that year, and Jane Deacy had told him there was an exciting part in the play for a young actor.

Dean mounted a long-term campaign in his efforts to win an audition. He knew that casting would not start until late summer or autumn, so on this first visit to the Ayers he concentrated on making himself a useful, personable, weekend guest. Rogers Brackett was certainly party to Dean's game, maybe even its instigator, for at this stage no mention was made of Dean being a budding young actor. Lemuel and Shirley Ayers decided they liked him, and invited him back for another weekend party. On this second visit Dean let it be known that he had had experience at sailing. No one bothered too much about the nature of his boating experience, and he was offered, as he had intended, a passage on the Ayers' yacht as an informal member of the crew.

It was only on the yacht, during a ten-day summer cruise, that Dean modestly revealed his acting ambitions, and Lemuel Ayers promised, as one friend to another, that Dean would be given a chance to audition for the new play. Again with the bisexual Ayers, it was claimed that Dean had a brief physical relationship of some sort – though beyond speculation there is no reason to believe that this ever happened. Dean's affectionate rapport with the Ayers children was a more probable bond between him and the family and the stepping-stone to that possible audition.

The occasional luxuries of life with the Ayers did not help solve the crisis of survival. The temporary let on Forty-sixth Street came to an end when the owners returned towards the end of September. Homeless and penniless once more Dean, Bill Bast, and the ex-UCLA girl joined forces with Dizzy Sheridan, the four of them taking a small and very sparsely furnished apartment in an old brownstone off Central Park in the West Eighties. They could borrow only the barest essentials of kitchen equipment and bedding, though the uncluttered floor space had one consolation for Dean, who chose the largest of the rooms as a bullring for his 'brownstone corridas'. He would take his practice cape and horns, and line up his room-mates as bulls, teaching them to charge the cape with the horns while he displayed his *veronicas*, *reboleras*, or *gaoneras*. It was a game he also used to play, with greater risk, in the city streets, using his jacket for a cape, and the yellow New York cabs as substitute bulls.

The uncomfortable conditions in the apartment, above all their permanent state of hunger, finally drove three of the brownstone friends out of the city. It was Dean's first 'surrender' in his twelve months of New York. On an apparent impulse he persuaded Bill Bast and Dizzy Sheridan to hitch-hike west with him to the farm in Indiana, as though he felt an instinctive need to re-establish some contact with a world beyond the claustrophobia of their frustrated ambitions.

The journey all but failed. It took a whole day waving their thumbs to reach the western end of the Pennsylvania turnpike, but during the night they made the remainder of the eight hundred miles in a single ride with a famous baseball player Clyde McCullough, 'catcher' for the Pittsburgh Pirates.

It was an auspicious start to their short vacation, and for the next few days the convalescence continued on the Winslow Farm. They slept in proper beds, were fed with huge meals, and abandoned themselves to the undemanding hospitality of Dean's uncle and aunt.

Dean dusted off his old motorbike and performed mad stunts for them up and down the country lanes. He showed off his uncle's cattle, and the steers he had helped to raise; and took them to visit the Rev De Weerd and his school drama coach, Adeline Nall. It was the first and only time that Bill Bast saw his friend back on home territory, identified again with that place of happy and unhappy memories, 'touching his roots', rebuilding his strength.

Dean's old high school honoured the three visitors by asking them to talk to the students. Briefly they played the unaccustomed role of celebrities, Dean lecturing on acting, Dizzy Sheridan on modern dance, Bast on television writing and directing. Bast recalls the awe of the school kids as very inappropriate, but a glorious boost to their three fragile morales.

Even Dean's father came out to see him, three thousand miles from Santa Monica, with a new bridge he had made for his son's missing front teeth.

When reality caught up with them it was in the form of a cable from Jane Deacy. Lemuel Ayers wanted Dean to audition for his forthcoming production of *See the Jaguar*, and the three friends hurried back to New York.

4. Broadway

Walk out on the tightrope. If the rope's hard
it's got to be leading somewhere.

James Dean

AUDITIONS for *See the Jaguar* had been underway for several weeks, and, although no final casting had been made, Dean knew there were several young actors on the short list for the part of the 'Jaguar', Wally Wilkins.

The play told the story of a teenager who had been shut away all his life by a protective and frightened mother. After the mother's death the boy comes out of his prison, a sixteen-year-old freak, illiterate, and wholly unprepared for the cruelties of the small town world in which he finds himself. The part was well suited to Dean, and the puzzled bewilderment he could project so convincingly.

On the day of the audition Dean was in a state of nervous paralysis, and his two room-mates had to calm him down and get him dressed. They met him after the audition. Bill Bast describes the scene:

We were halfway there when we saw him walking slowly down the street towards us. We stopped, afraid to know the answer, and tried to determine from his expression what had happened. His face told the story. No one said a word. We just stood there on the street corner, laughing and crying like three crazy, grateful little kids. After many intense months of clinging to a slippery handful of faith and hope, the slightest part of a dream come true can be an exalting experience.

For the first time in his professional life Dean had a long, serious part in which to immerse himself, an adequate amount of time for rehearsal and, above all, a director whom he respected and trusted (Michael Gordon). The disappointments of the television studios could for the moment be forgotten as he observed and participated in the craftsmanship of his fellow actors – in particular the lead star, Arthur Kennedy, another product of the Actors Studio.

Dean would return home to the brownstone apartment in the evenings full of the excitement of the day's rehearsals, acting out for his room-mates each of the main parts in the play and explaining to them the subtleties of Gordon's staging. He had mastered his lines within a few days, but experienced more trouble with the song he had to sing in the play: a little folk tune written by his friend Alec Wilder especially for the production, 'Green Briar, Blue Fire'. Being practically tone-deaf Dean had a terrible time trying to learn the tune. He was intensely self-conscious of his singing and would only practise in a dark room at dead of night, to the amusement but eventual despair of his flatmates.

Rehearsals went smoothly until they moved out of town into Connecticut for trial previews. Then, during one of the final run-throughs in the theatre at Hartford, Dean had a fight with one of the stage-hands and ending up pulling a switchblade on him. It was apparently Arthur Kennedy who broke up the fight, not without some harsh words for his young co-star. The incident could have been a simple quarrel, a stage-hand's ill-timed remark; it could have been an accumulation of nervous tension; it could even have been a calculated moment of self-triggering by Dean, trying perhaps to spark off some detail of insight or invention within his role as Wally Wilkins. In an impasse Dean needed adrenalin as badly as some actors need liquor. Two years later, when they were working together on *Rebel Without a Cause,* he would tell Dennis Hopper à propos of the mechanics of

invention: 'When you know there's something more to go in the character and you're not sure what it is, you just got to go out after it. Walk out on the tightrope. If the rope's hard it's got to be leading somewhere.'

See the Jaguar opened in New York at the Cort Theatre on 3 December 1952. The first night audience responded well to the play and afterwards, at the celebration in Sardi's, Dean was triumphant. He took Bill Bast and Dizzy Sheridan to the party with him, and they remembered him, flying round the room from table to table, soaking up the praise, talking and joking with everyone.

It was a strange night for the two people who had shared so much of his struggle and disappointment. Dizzy was aware that the play had swept Dean into a different existence from the life on the outside, where they had been able to help each other. At the party she felt like a hanger-on. Bill Bast had arrived at the theatre in an understandable confusion of pride and envy. He and Dean had, after all, started out as equals: 'I was stunned by the realisation that at no time during the performance had I been aware that I was watching my friend James Dean. He had so completely created an illusion for me and the rest of the audience that I had believed in Wally Wilkins, the part he was playing, not Jimmy Dean, the boy I knew.'

But the party at Sardi's ended in gloom when the morning papers arrived. The play had been condemned by most of the critics as naive and over-symbolic. It was to close after only six performances, and Dean's bitter disappointment was mollified only by the way his own performance had been singled out for special praise. Walter Kerr, in the *New York Herald Tribune,* wrote:

> James Dean adds an extraordinary performance in an almost impossible role: that of a bewildered lad who has been completely shut off from a vicious world by an over-zealous mother, and who is coming upon both the beauty and brutality of the mountain for the first time.

In See the Jaguar

This Broadway debut, however ephemeral, marked the major

turning point in Dean's acting career. The play had been a good showcase for him and his performance had attracted enough attention in the six days to change his status in casting offices. From this point on Jane Deacy was able to shape her client's career, rejecting the kind of bit parts with which he had been surviving during the previous year and concentrating instead on young character parts, and 'juvenile' supporting roles.

There were an increasing number of these roles available. The 'hep teenager' was creeping into contemporary drama, the young television writers of the day influenced on one level by the emergence of the Kerouac-style wanderers, the first of the hippie-beats; and on another level by the cynical alienation of Salinger's Holden Caulfield from *The Catcher in the Rye*, the problem teenager from East Coast city affluence.

Not that the sponsored television series could concern themselves very often with such straight drama. The titles of some of Dean's work that year speak for themselves: *Hound of Heaven, The Case of the Sawed-off Shotgun, Life Sentence, A Long Time Till Dawn, Death is My Neighbour, Sentence of Death.* One week he would be a confused murderer on the run, holed up in a lonely house, another week, a 'hep-cat' killer; in September a mentally unbalanced young janitor in an apartment block, in November his first 'starring' role, a violent hoodlum regressed to childhood (*A Long Time Till Dawn*). From the little we know of the content of his work, it seems he was cast most often for his portrayals of vulnerable, frustrated youth, or psychotic unease.

He became one of three top young actors competing for the juvenile leads at that time, the others, not surprisingly, being Paul Newman and Steve McQueen. The three of them must have seen as much as they could stomach of each other, hanging around the casting offices, or queuing for auditions.

If they had been competing on a league basis Dean would have been out in front during that year, and his success at picking up the better parts was due more than anything else to the audience reaction he inspired. The Schurr office would have made programme sponsors aware of the fan mail: rave letters from young girls, brotherly letters from young boys, pornographic letters from old ladies and gentlemen. The scale of response was nothing to compare with the deluge that followed his first feature film, but it was already an indication of the magnetic strength of his screen personality.

Hardly any material has survived from the television dramas in which he took part. In those years there was little attempt made to preserve TV material; the shows went out live and the hungry monster ate and digested. Only later, when Dean became a major movie star, did the companies and sponsors begin to retain his shows for repeat screening. To form any opinion of his work at this time we have to rely on what little his contemporaries remember.

His output was certainly uneven. In the conveyor-belt frenzy of the television studios a good script and a good director counted for everything. Dean was an explorative actor, an experimenter. In rehearsal he would never play a scene twice the same way, to the despair and often the fury of his fellow actors. A good director would give him the room to explore a role in this way, watching his changing interpretations and freezing him when he found the correct one. A bad director would either sit on him too hard or leave him to his wanderings and lose him. They would end up either with a performance full of mannerism or a disjointed interpretation unintegrated with the rest of the piece.

Apart from the quality of his acting on television, his reputation as a worker is also difficult to assess. People seemed to react to him on set the same way his friends and enemies reacted to him outside. They either liked him or they hated him. One can find few neutrals in Dean's world.

Perhaps the actress Mary Astor was one of the neutrals, an affectionate, good-humoured neutral. She worked with James Dean on a 'US Steel Hour' drama called *The*

Thief and remembered the occasion in her autobiography, *A Life on Film*:

We were doing a final dress rehearsal: 'from the top – no stops, please'. Jimmy was six feet away from me in one scene and I could barely hear what he was saying, and what I could hear seemed to have very little to do with the script. I looked over at the booth, my palms up in a 'Help!' gesture.

'What's the trouble, Mary?' asked the director, his voice booming impatiently over the loudspeaker. Paul Lukas, that excellent actor, came to my rescue.

He said, 'De trouble iss dat ve don't know vat de hell he's saying, ven he's going to say vat, or vere he's goint to be ven he says anything.' You could understand Paul.

Our answer came over the loudspeaker. 'I'm sorry people. That's the way Jimmy has to work. Do the best you can. It's marvellous in here.'

Paul mumbled in excellent imitation of Jimmy: 'So for Chrissakes get us some earphones too!'

'What's that Paul?'

'Oh, notting. I vas just vishing I could be marvellous too.'

We exchanged twinkling appreciative looks feeling superior to this newcomer, this young whippersnapper (vippersnopper). We were experienced, we had a sense of responsibility to each other; we knew how to be co-operative, not only with each other but also with technicians, conscious that they too had a job. Experience is apt to make one feel superior; unfortunately it also makes us prejudiced. We become rigid, all-of-a-piece. 'This works, this is right, this is the way it's done – the only way.'

Jimmy Dean, that vippersnopper, in his quiet thoughtful mumbling way got the notices. Paul and I were 'also in the cast'.

Critical appreciation of television drama was, as it still is, uneven and arbitrary. It was difficult for any play to be sure of notices even in the trade press, and when a comparatively unknown actor was singled out for praise the name was registered in casting offices on both sides of the continent.

CBS-TV exec-producer William Dozier brought in two top stars, Sir Cedric Hardwicke and Walter Hampden, for his Tuesday night crime block, *Suspense* and *Danger*, last week, but a newcomer, James Dean, stole the spotlight from both of them. Dean, cast with Hampden on *Danger* in the role of a psychotic young janitor, delivered a magnetic performance that brought a routine meller alive.

Dean's performance was in many ways reminiscent of Marlon Brando's in *Streetcar*, but he gave the role the individuality and nuances of its own which it required. He's got quite a future ahead of him.

This notice in a September issue of *Variety* helped prompt an offer for a general audition from MGM. Jane Deacy advised Dean against taking up the offer. She was determined that her client would make the step into feature films, not with the usual general studio contract but on the strength of a good part in a suitably prestigious movie.

Her instinct for the right and wrong parts can be judged on the specific movie offers that were made during this year. The first role offered to Dean from a Hollywood studio was the lead in a major costume epic, *The Silver Chalice*, the sheer size and scale of which would have persuaded most actors and agents. Jane Deacy held off the offer. The script was weak, and the part Dean had to play ill-defined. Her judgement was later proved correct. The film was a flop, and the role that Dean would have played did nothing to further the career of the young actor who eventually accepted it, Paul Newman. Ten years later when *The Silver Chalice* was released on television, Newman took advertising space to apologise both for the film and his own performance.

Of the two auditions Dean did try for, only one would have brought him any success: the part of Curly in the musical *Oklahoma*. Perhaps it was just as well that Dean failed to persuade Zinnemann of his potential as a singer; the Dean image might not have absorbed such a frivolous adventure.

Dean's second audition was for the Raoul Walsh war epic, *Battle Cry*, and if the studio had not insisted on a recognised 'box-office' name (Tab Hunter) he would have been picked to play the part of Danny. It was another escape, for the film was not a critical success and no performance from Dean could have salvaged it. (Both *Battle Cry* and *The Silver Chalice* were shooting in the Warners' studios when Dean arrived in Hollywood the next year, and he was a regular visitor on the sets: on *Battle Cry* to watch his old tutor James Whitmore at work; and on *The Silver Chalice* to admire Paul Newman's co-star, Pier Angeli.)

Auditions apart Dean's work was concentrated, during that autumn and early winter of 1953, on his growing success as a television star. There was no shortage of work for him and his roles were increasing in size and importance (*Death is My Neighbour*, *The Big Story*, *Keep Our Honour Bright*, *Life Sentence*, *A Long Time Till Dawn*, *The Bells of Cockaigne*, *Harvest*). By the time he was cast for his second Broadway play at the end of the year, his name was acquiring what the business liked to call 'box-office potential'.

Dean's professional success during this year had meant changes in his New York way of life. The trio of friends in the brownstone apartment broke up during the weeks that followed his Broadway debut in *See the Jaguar*. Dizzy Sheridan had accepted an offer of work abroad, perhaps a deliberate move away from Dean and the city in which they had shared a year of their lives. She took up a professional dancing job in Trinidad and when she left town Bill Bast moved into a friend's apartment. Dean returned to the Iroquois Hotel.

These were weeks of withdrawal and isolation for Dean; a pattern of behaviour that seems to have followed each successful period of work: as though the work itself had drained him or the completion of it convinced him in some way of its ultimate irrelevance. We know that acting never wholly satisfied his need of self-expression; that he was determined one day to progress to directing and even to writing. The end of work on a play or a film usually produced a reaction of gloomy dissatisfaction, a mood of withdrawal to be followed by intense mental activity or in later days by the irresistible urge to race motorcars.

Bill Bast moved back into the Iroquois a few weeks after Dean and found his friend immersed in a course of reading and music study. An actor friend, Frank Corsaro, had introduced him to Huxley and Schönberg; he had met a young American composer, Leonard Rosenman (who would later write the scores for both *East of Eden* and *Rebel Without a Cause*). Having found new subjects and new teachers Dean had latched onto them with all his old thirst for learning. He even bought himself an English flute (bass recorder) and was teaching himself to play with the help of one of his older 'tutors'.

When Bast left New York for a television writing job in Los Angeles, the three books Dean gave to him as a leaving present were his current oracles: Virginia Woolf's *Orlando*; Carson McCullers' *The Heart is a Lonely Hunter*; and *The Andre Maurois Reader*. In the Maurois book Dean had written a message of encouragement:

> To Bill – While in the aura of metaphysical whoo-haas, ebb away your displeasures on this. May flights of harpies escort your wingéd trip of vengeance.

The television work that accumulated during that year gave Dean financial security he had

'I mean no one walked like that in those days'

never previously known. But his life-style changed very little. He never bought himself clothes and never frequented expensive bars or restaurants. His only luxuries were books, gramophone records and the motorbike which he'd had sent out from the farm in Fairmount. Otherwise his daily round was much the same as before, centring, as with most of the young radio and TV actors, on the Cromwell's coffee bar downstairs in the RCA building, the sorting house for gossip, casting news or new friendships. He was becoming by now a recognised figure on the New York scene. Film director Joe Massot was a teenager in Greenwich Village at the time: 'A lot of people knew about him from his television work. That charisma was already working and not just his acting. Even if people didn't know who he was they'd turn and look at him walking down the street. I mean no one walked like that in those days.'

Dean was adopted by numerous friends or 'acquaintances' in Cromwell's or Walgreen's, or at the Algonquin where he sometimes spent his evenings. Some of them were little more than camp followers, the sycophants and spongers that Dean could never quite shake off. Not that he ever seemed troubled by them. He had a disconcerting habit of totally ignoring anyone who was either boring or annoying him: a freezing off of any sort of communication which was even inflicted on close friends whenever he was depressed or withdrawn.

He made fewer and fewer concessions to conventional behaviour, drifting in and out of people's lives apparently at will and random. He would call unannounced, and sometimes sit for hours in a friend's house without speaking. At other times he could be the clowning life and soul of any gathering; extempore champion of the absurd, like the day he carried an armchair down four flights of stairs to sit himself in the middle of a busy New York street.

Night or day he would walk the city, watching, listening and learning. He would talk for hours with cabbies and waitresses, the news-stand operators, his old friend 'Moondog', the blind musician who wandered the New York streets – or a newer and younger friend, met over breakfast one morning, fellow-actor Jonathan Gilmour. Jonathan's recollections of homosexual Hollywood were similar to Dean's. They'd both been 'pretty boys' in LA, hustling or hustled, Gilmour younger than Dean but with a longer list of credits from his former juvenile roles. His impression of James Dean at this time is of a young man freeing himself from any kind of social or personal inhibition; an artist opening himself to any passing image or idea; the actor ready to lose himself in the lives that passed him on the streets or in the bars – taking Gilmour to a Greenwich Village fancy-dress party, both of them in drag, and later, a rather drunken evening of affectionate if ultimately unsuccessful sexual exploration between the two of them. Both young men were attracted to one another, Jonathan perhaps less ready to lose ingrained inhibitions than the friend he came to call 'the explorer'. For Dean wanted to absorb everything and everybody, good and bad, the whole technicolor pageant, his collection of characters and emotions sometimes strung out behind him, the Pied Piper – at other times instead, crowded uncomfortably and uneasily inside his head.

Dean appeared Pied Piper also with his girls, though this time without apparent serious purpose or commitment. That was almost the precondition, his rule. The relationship with Dizzy Sheridan had been a supportive feature of his first year in New York, Dizzy herself adapting easily to his fluctuating moods and to their financial circumstances. But even they had shied away from too strong a dependence on one another, and whatever passion they may have shared in the early days did not inhibit

At home: West Sixty-eighth Street, New York.

what also became a close friendship, still warm but usually relaxed. Not that Dean was undemanding of his friends. At times he seemed to require (and often test) their total and unconditional loyalty. Love and dependence were emotions Dean could not easily cope with, either in himself or in other people – an almost inevitable consequence of the loss of his mother and the close relationship they had shared: love is everything but love can be taken away, therefore it is dangerous.

Even Bill Bast could not keep track of the endless parade of girls that had followed Dizzy Sheridan:

> He would run into a new face in the Schurr office, or at Walgreen's, or at Cromwell's, and attach himself to her for a few hours, or, at the most, a day. The girls would accompany him wherever he went: to his agent's office, or interviews, to rehearsals, to dinner, on walks, or to his room.

Not surprisingly the only two girls who maintained any sort of lasting relationship with him during this year were both actresses: Chris White, with whom he had auditioned at the Actors Studio; and Barbara Glenn, who had met him in Cromwell's when *See the Jaguar* was opening on Broadway.

Dean's liaison with Barbara Glenn, intermittent and stormy though it appears to have been, was one of the reasons behind his eventual decision to move out of the Iroquois and find his own apartment. Girls were not permitted in the hotel rooms. Dean took a set of rooms in an elderly building on West Sixty-eighth Street. Apart from the house he later rented as a Hollywood base for the last months of his life, this New York den became the one real home he made for himself outside of Fairmount. Film director Nicholas Ray described it in a later visit: 'There was no elevator. A fairly large plainly-furnished room with two port-hole windows, a studio couch, a table, some unmatching chairs and stools; on the wall a bullfighting poster, capes and horns; everywhere piles of books and records, some neatly stacked, some precarious or spilling over. A door led to the kitchen and bathroom, another to

As Bachir the arab boy in
The Immoralist

a flight of stairs by which one reached the roof. It was evening. The only light came from the fireplace, scrap wood and boxes burning. The records: African tribal music, Afro-Cuban songs and dances, classical jazz, Jack Teagarden, Dave Brubeck, Haydn, Berlioz…'

The dance and rhythm music belonged to two new activities in Dean's life which he took up during his second year in New York: dancing, which he began studying with Katherine Dunham; and the bongo drums he was learning to play in the Greenwich Village cellars.

The dancing was an exercise on his part to achieve greater physical flexibility in his acting and lose the inhibited stiffness that apparently marked some of his television performances. On a cramped TV set movement could not be expressed with too much exuberance, and the only alternative, in Dean's opinion, was to learn the more controlled expressions of modern dance or ballet.

He was soon able to apply his dancing techniques directly to his acting. In November or December 1953, Dean auditioned for a part in a Billy Rose production, *The Immoralist*. The play was an adaptation by Ruth and Augustus Goetz from the André Gide novel: the story of a French archaeologist (Louis Jourdan in the play) on honeymoon with his young wife (Geraldine Page), and how the marriage breaks up under the strain of his homosexuality.

Dean was auditioning for the part of the corrupt young Arab house-boy who tempts Jourdan back into his adolescent homosexuality by introducing him to a male Arab prostitute. In one scene of the play the house-boy dances for Jourdan and this was the scene Dean insisted on playing at the audition, with apparent success.

There were high hopes for this production, and Dean felt justified in turning down any more television work while he prepared for the role. When rehearsals were postponed two weeks he took advantage of the interval to spend some days with his family in Indiana. It was more than a year since he had been home, and he had missed any chance of a summer vacation due to his television work. The only relaxation he had taken that year had been a short and disastrous spell crewing the Ayers yacht in an ocean-going regatta: he had been seasick from start to finish.

To the great consternation of his future producer and director he decided to make the journey to Indiana by motorbike. The original motorbike sent out to him from the farm had been changed several times during the year. Each time Dean's television fees had been raised he had bought a bigger and faster machine. That December he was riding an English Triumph 500, and there were friends and interested parties in New York who believed they would never see him again when he set out on it into the snow-bound midwinter interior of the continent.

He made the eight hundred miles in two days of riding and spent a week on the farm, walking and shooting in the fields and reading T. E. Lawrence's *Seven Pillars of Wisdom*. By the time he arrived back in New York, he had developed his own strong ideas about the Arab part he had to play.

The Immoralist was well on into rehearsal before any friction started, and Dean had by then established a good rapport with the director Herman Schulman. Schulman had been receptive to Dean's suggestions about playing the part for its tragic undertones, and Dean's acting in rehearsal had already attracted praise from his co-star Geraldine Page. But when they opened an out-of-town preview in Philadelphia, Billy Rose was not happy with the results and called in Daniel Mann to replace Schulman, restage the show and supervise some rewriting.

The Philadelphia reviews had been very good, and Dean was confused and upset by the sudden changes. His own part as the Arab boy had been singled out for special praise and now he found the part shrinking with each day's rehearsing. Nor was there any time for tact or sympathy. The show had to transfer onto Broadway within a week. Val Holley quotes Daniel Mann's own description of Dean rehearsing: 'Like a fox fucking a football – he's all around it but can't get in.'

Apparently Billy Rose felt the play had become heavy and too over-laden with tragedy. He wanted some light relief, and Dean's part was the obvious vehicle for a few laughs. Those people who saw the play in Philadelphia had praised the subtlety of Dean's interpretation, a straight and rather menacing picture of sexual ambivalence; though it seems possible, especially after his immersion into Lawrence, that he had over-played the dramatic or tragic aspects of the role.

Wherever the blame and whatever the faults, tension and friction finally climaxed in a showdown between Dean and Mann only a day or so before the New York opening. Dean asked a question, and Daniel Mann rounded on him: 'What makes you think you're so important here?' The row had been brewing all week, and in the heat of the moment Dean walked out of the theatre. When he had cooled down enough to come back he found the rehearsal progressing with his understudy playing for him (the black actor Billy Gunn). A diplomatic intervention by an Equity official, and apparently some strong pressure from Geraldine Page, restored Dean to the cast and the play opened as planned.

But Dean's commitment to the play was now lost. He believed the changes had cheapened the drama and bitterly resented the way he had been steamrollered by Daniel Mann. *The Immoralist* opened at the Royale Theatre on 1 February 1954, and on that first night, a night of triumph both for Dean and for the play, he handed in his two weeks' notice to quit.

Both audience and critics had given the play a good reception and Dean won the last laugh over the director, a mild thumbing of his nose at the way his part had been camped up in the alterations: at his curtain-call he stepped forward, lifted up his robe, and curtsied. While his performance that night, curtsy and all, would earn him a mention as one of the most promising newcomers in the *Theatre World* yearbook, the audience reception was particularly gratifying for Dean since his uncle and aunt had come out from Indiana to be present at the opening night. Dean had told them nothing about the quarrels that had led up to his decision to quit, and the two of them returned to Fairmount having seen Jimmy at one of his rare peaks, prince of Broadway and Manhattan for one brief evening.

Most of his friends were now telling him to retract his decision to quit. The play was sure to have a long run, and a quarrel with the management could only damage his reputation. They warned him he would end up one day with no one prepared to employ him.

Dean ignored the advice and shut himself away for the remainder of his two weeks' work on the show; intransigent, moody, unapproachable. Though he didn't yet know it himself, his obstinacy was about to reap an unexpected reward.

Elia Kazan had arrived in New York from his country home in Connecticut, where he had been working on a film script with Paul Osborn: an adaptation of John Steinbeck's latest novel *East of Eden*. Jean Deacy saw the script and realised that the central role in the film

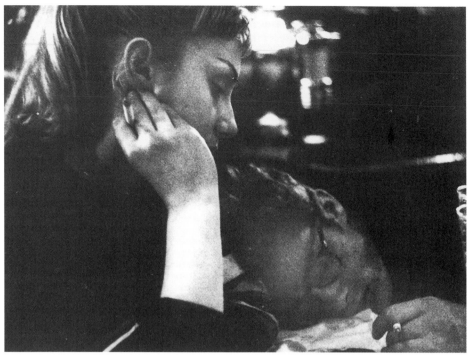

In New York Jerry's bar on West Fifty-fourth was one of Jimmy's favourite places to hang out.

was entirely suited to Dean's temperament and his acting gifts. She asked Kazan to visit the Royale before Dean's two weeks' notice had expired.

As events turned out it was Paul Osborn who saw *The Immoralist* on one of Dean's last evenings in the play, and telephoned Kazan next morning to recommend Dean for the part of Cal. Kazan asked Dean round to Warners' New York office. He had had some contact with Dean at the Actors Studio the year before but knew very little about him, either as an actor or as a person. He had no strong feelings or instincts about him, beyond a general antipathy towards his surly, rebellious attitudes. There was certainly none of the instant 'chemistry' he had experienced in his early meetings with Brando. Dean seems to have given his usual slouching, surly performance in the office – Kazan later said 'utterly without charm'.

But as he talked with Dean – in the office, in Dean's apartment or riding round town with him on the motorbike – Kazan realised that there were so many elements in Dean's own life similar to the character in *East of Eden*. Dean's mood at that time, the anger and obstinacy over the play, only strengthened Kazan's impressions. Dean was sent to meet Steinbeck, whose impression was much the same: he didn't like the young man, but in looks and behaviour Dean *was* Cal Trask.

The casting in *East of Eden* depended on various degrees of compatibility, friction, and contrast between the three young leads: two brothers, and a girlfriend. Originally there had been talk of Marlon Brando and Montgomery Clift playing the two brothers; but by the time auditions were being filmed in New York the short list of contenders had been narrowed down to Richard Davalos, Paul Newman, and James Dean; with Joanne Woodward or Julie Harris for the girl. Brando had probably been excluded for contractual reasons: he was in the middle of a protracted row with Twentieth Century Fox over his refusal to work on *The Egyptian* and was unlikely to be released or loaned to work at Warner's. Whether Clift was ever seriously considered is not clear. Certainly the combination of the two of them would have made the brothers seem a lot older than was intended in either the book or the script, where the two of them are still schoolboys.

The same argument might have applied to Paul Newman, then twenty-nine years old to Dean's twenty-three. Whatever the criteria, various combinations were tried in screen tests, including one session between James Dean and Paul Newman – the occasion when Dean ad-libbed the line on camera at Newman, 'Kiss me.' 'I didn't hear that,' Paul Newman replied with an uneasy grin. The two of them might have worked well together and Newman would undoubtedly have portrayed a more complex and sympathetic Aron. Instead the decision was made to cast Dean with Davalos and Julie Harris. Dean had won himself the choice Hollywood role of that year and with a director already famous for his acting discoveries.

Preparations and filming were to take place in California, and Dean intended to make the four-thousand-mile trip across the continent on his motorbike. But a few days before leaving he had a bad spill on the bike and Kazan told him to shut it away until the film was over.

Dean packed his few necessaries in an untidy bundle, said goodbye to his New York friends and took the airplane to Los Angeles with Kazan – Dean's first trip in a airplane and the start of a legendary, if tragically short-lived, film career.

5. East of Eden

They've brought out from New York another
dirty-shirt-tail actor. If this is the kind of
talent they're importing, they can send it right
back again so far as I'm concerned.

Hedda Hopper, 1954

I sat spellbound in the projection room. I
couldn't remember ever having seen a young
man with so much power, so many facets of
expression, so much sheer invention.

Hedda Hopper, 1955

THAT SPRING of 1954, audiences were queuing to see *The Glenn Miller Story*; the
successful pop songs were innocuous matinee tunes, 'Doggie in the Window','The
Happy Wanderer', 'Stranger in Paradise'. In New York Toscanini had announced his
retirement. In Hollywood Audrey Hepburn had won her Oscar. Billy Graham was on his
way to London, Marilyn Monroe to the hundred thousand marines left behind in Korea. In
the White House, Eisenhower was drafting his message of encouragement to the besieged
French Army at Bien Dien Phu in Vietnam, and, on Capitol Hill, an ever more ambitious
McCarthy was lining up the whole United States Army in his inquisitorial sights.

The anti-Communist witch-hunt had already carved its swathe of destruction through
the American cinema. In the voluntary exodus that followed, Hollywood had lost, among
many others, Bertolt Brecht, Fritz Lang, Joseph Losey, Carl Foreman, John Huston, and
Orson Welles. And a few weeks before James Dean's arrival in Hollywood, Mike Connelly
was writing in the *Hollywood Reporter*: 'Wonderful to wash our hands of those dreary
Chaplins, even tho' he did make a lousy 20 million dollar fortune here. It's almost worth it
to be rid of such crumbums.'

This was the Hollywood Dean remembered from two years previously, with its
establishment jingoism and self-perpetuating glitter and glamour. He had had his own
worm's-eye view of that world and his memories were ugly with humiliation and self-
abasement. He knew too intimately the abuses of power, the exploitation of hopeful young
talent. He had also watched young movie stars manipulated by the publicity offices and
forced into roles and images over which they had little or no control. In his intervening
two years in New York he had developed himself as a serious actor: he had played lead
roles in television drama, and his two stage performance on Broadway had been well

received. He now felt that he had earned his return to Hollywood, and he was determined to live and work there strictly on his own terms.

After arriving in Los Angeles, Kazan told Dean that he needed a suntan and some flesh on his bones for the character he was about to portray. Dean had about two weeks before tests and rehearsals began, and called his old friend Bill Bast, who knew of a place in Borrego Springs where they could stay. Dean hired a car and the two old friends vanished out into the California desert, stopping there for nearly a week while Dean gathered his thoughts and organised his attitudes before facing the maelstrom of Hollywood. They were not attitudes that would endear him to conventional 'showbiz'.

On the day they arrived back in town from Borrego Springs, they went to visit Dick Clayton of Famous Artists, the agent looking after Dean's interests in Hollywood. While they were talking, another agent came breezing into the room, shouting for a secretary. Dean told the man to get out. 'You come in here, braying like an ass when we're in the middle of a conference. Haven't you got any manners?' Later, when they left the building, Dean laughed about his outburst. 'That loud-mouthed slob. Four years ago he gave me a hard time on an interview here.'

Forgetting and forgiving did not come easy to him. He would always regard achievement and especially his own achievement as a hard won victory against the odds, a victory in which there was little room for gratitude or feelings of obligation. That first day back in Hollywood, Bast and Dean met up with another new arrival from New York, Paul Newman. Newman told Dean, 'I wanted that part in *Eden* so bad I could taste it.' Paul Newman turned to Bast. 'Bill, so help me, every time I went to read for a part in New York this clown would be there. Got so's I couldn't turn around without seeing him. Lucky breaks,' Newman said, 'that's what an actor's life is all about.' Dean disagreed, and when Bast and Newman tried to make him admit that he had had help along the way, Dean lost his temper and thumped the table. 'No one ever did anything for me. I did it myself. I don't owe anything to anyone.'

Whatever his reservations about Hollywood Dean abandoned himself freely enough to the normal trappings of success during those early weeks. Dick Clayton obtained an advance from Warners on Dean's $20,000 fee, and Kazan's latest discovery was soon to be seen down Sunset Boulevard in a red MG sports car, touring the traditional night spots with a succession of pretty young starlets, his only claim to notoriety the scruffy blue jeans that excluded him from the smarter clubs and restaurants. Though Dean was soon to buy himself a new motorbike, his contract with Warners included a specific ban on riding motorcycles until work was completed on *East of Eden*. By way of compensation he bought a palomino horse and kept it at a ranch near to town, where he would spend hours riding or just leaning over the corral watching it.

The ranch became one of his few hideaways, where he could temporarily escape the attentions of photographers or columnists anxious to record the off-guard comments of this new Garfield-Clift-Brando rebel. The elder Burbank statesmen dismissed his unconventional attitudes as being nothing more than a Warners' gimmick for publicists. After all, his scruffy clothes and scornful, surly attitudes did not fit in with the comfortable playboy's life he was giving himself.

Those who had known Dean in the earlier years had different opinions. Nick Adams, who had worked with him on the Pepsi-Cola commercial in 1951: 'Jimmy was most of the time straight with himself. He'd never known the good time and he wanted to see what it was like. It was the only way he knew of deciding how much he was going to accept of all the movie star bit. Once they started working he made his own way of life. And whatever didn't fit into it he dropped.'

Cal in his bean field. 'The American farm boy with the eyes of an injured animal.'

East of Eden is an adaptation of the last third of John Steinbeck's novel and is set in the Salinas Valley, California, at the time of the First World War. James Dean was to play the younger of two motherless brothers (twins in the novel), both dominated in different ways by their puritanical father (Raymond Massey) and representing quite clearly their biblical counterparts, Cain and Abel. The elder brother, Aron (Richard Davalos), is the model son, apple of his father's eye, a good student at high school and going steady with a sweet local girl, Abra (Julie Harris). James Dean's Cal (Cain) is the black sheep, cutting school, roaming the countryside, picking up girls, drinking. His father's puritan severity repudiates the badness in the boy, and Cal's love for his father seems doomed to misunderstanding and rejection.

Cal finds his supposedly dead mother running a whore-house in the seaside town of Monterey. The mother (Jo Van Fleet) refuses to see him, and has him frightened off by a bouncer. Cal returns home, quarrels with his father, but promises never to mention the mother to his brother. A family friend, the sheriff (Burl Ives) tells him the full story of his parents' quarrel, how his mother shot his father, and fled from the monotony of life on a ranch.

Cal makes a new effort to get on with his father, joining Aron in helping on their father's experimental project, harvesting Salinas Valley lettuce and sending it in refrigerated railcars to the eastern markets. But the project fails and the father's money is lost. Determined to set things right on his own, Cal borrows $5,000 from his mother and secretly invests in bean crops. The US is about to enter the war in Europe, and the price of beans will go 'sky-high'.

The war arrives, and Aron, a pacifist, is deeply disturbed by the implications. Already there is tension between Aron, Abra and Cal, as the mutual attraction between Cal and Abra becomes more and more obvious. Cal sells off the bean crop investment, making a profit, and for his father's birthday gives him back the money that he lost on the refrigeration experiment. But his father rejects the gift, rejoicing instead in the announcement of Aron's engagement to Abra. In a fit of jealous rage Cal drags Aron off to Monterey and confronts him in the whore-house with his long-lost mother.

'Cain rose up against Abel his brother,
and slew him.'

Aron's tidy and self-satisfied way of life is shattered. Spurning his pacifism he joins the army and goes off to war, leaving his father literally heart-broken with grief. Cal and Abra are left alone to nurse him and with the help of the girl, father and son are in some measure reconciled.

'And Cain went out from the presence
of the Lord and dwelt in the land of
Nod on the east of Eden.'

James Dean did not find it difficult to identify with the part of Cal. Though his childhood and adolescence had not been unhappy, he had never re-established a close relationship with his father after his mother's death. He had known the extremes of loneliness and had felt rejection; and, like Cal, he believed himself marked in some way by abnormality or badness.

Nor were these parallels between James Dean and Cal Trask accidental. Kazan had been well aware of them when he had chosen Dean for the part. 'I cast Jimmy because he was Cal. There was no point in attempting to cast it better. Jimmy was it. He had a grudge against all fathers. He was vengeful; he had a sense of aloneness and of being persecuted; and he was suspicious.'

But the film, and in particular the role of Cal, were personal also to Elia Kazan, and his close identification with theme and character had a significant effect on his relationship with James Dean. 'What attracted me [to *East of Eden*] was nothing very mysterious: the story of a son trying to please his father who disapproved of him was one part of it. Another part of it was an opportunity for me to attack puritanism; the absolute puritanism of "this is right and this is wrong". I was trying to show that right and wrong get mixed up and that there are values that have to be looked at more deeply than in that absolute approval or disapproval syndrome of my left friends.'

Elia Kazan had been in the centre of the unhappy McCarthy stage three years previously. A former Communist Party member, he was one of the few left-wing 'liberals' to co-operate with the Senate Committee, naming colleagues and friends who had been in the party with him, and his defection had left great bitterness on both sides. His latest film *On the Waterfront* had dealt, in a somewhat confused and heroic way, with the similar theme of a young man testifying against a corrupt trade union. And now, in *East of Eden*, this political memory was never far below the surface.

The film was also personally autobiographical for Kazan. The whole relationship between father and son had echoes from his own life and he identified strongly with the malice and anger of the central (Dean) character. 'When I was young I was full of anger. I looked like a hungry wolf; I was thin, my eyes were close together and I wouldn't look at anybody. I look at pictures of myself then and I can see the resentment, the hatred towards everybody… It was autobiographical, that picture – more personal than anything I've ever done. There's some disguise, some transfers, but I know every feeling in that picture. That's why it is very pure. You like it or you don't, but what's being said there is heartfelt. That was the first picture, I feel, that started this talking about myself through film-making.'

Father (Raymond Massey) and son momentarily reconciled as they work on the lettuce harvest (above); Cal nursing his secret – the bean field that will pay his father's debts (below).

Elia Kazan and Julie Harris shooting the train sequence when Cal crosses the mountains to Monterey.

This strong personal identification helps explain Kazan's close hold on Dean throughout the preparation and making of the film. He was determined to shape the part his own way, and his approach was altogether different from the partnership he had adopted with Brando, when they had explored their respective ways to the interpretations of Stanley Kowalski in *A Streetcar Named Desire*, Zapata in *Viva Zapata!* and Terry Malloy in *On the Waterfront.* A lesser director than Kazan might have failed to pull Dean along with him, since Dean was also drawing – and more directly, since he was the actor – from his own emotional life. That Kazan did manage to control Dean was due more than anything else to the close rapport he established from the very beginning. Bill Bast had been present at one of the early pre-production meetings:

> Kazan and Jimmy joked and kidded about everything in general. There was a warm, easy harmony between them, the seasoned artist, and his younger disciple. I saw no evidence of the usual director-actor relationship, but felt instead that they were simply old friends. When it came time for serious words on the picture they went into a huddle and discussed their plans in muffled tones. Kazan had created a strong feeling of intimacy and exclusivity in his relationship with Jimmy, keeping their exchange esoteric at all times.

At Kazan's suggestion Dean and Richard Davalos shared accommodation during preparation and rehearsals. They took a small apartment across the road from Warners'

Studios and lived the love-hate reality of their respective parts as the good and bad brothers.

The preparation worked perfectly. They were both new to the celebrity game, feeling their way through the farrago of publicity and production. They were sharing the experience as brothers, helping each other through it, but at the same time competing in a natural way for sympathy and attention. When filming finally got underway the tensions in their screen relationship had become instinctive.

Shooting on the picture started on 27 May out in the California countryside at Mendocino (the Monterey location), moving on to Salinas on 4 June. The work on exterior locations gave Dean the space and latitude to find the physical reality of the character he was playing – what Herbert Kretzmer later described in the *Daily Sketch* as: 'The American farm boy with the eyes of an injured animal… the innocent grace of a captive panther.'

The early location work was also a period of discovery for Kazan, as he evaluated his new young actor: '…His face was very poetic. I think his face was wonderful and very painful. You really feel so sorry for him when you see him in close-up; but I realised there was great value in his body. His body was more expressive, actually, than Brando's – it had so much tension in it. Brando has terrific tension, but he has great strength in being static… Dean had a very vivid body; and I did play a lot with it in long shots. And Cinemascope emphasised Dean's smallness. When he runs in the bean fields: there's a big thing like that, wide, and you see Dean running through it, looking like a little child.'

The opening sequences of the film establish that strong physical presence, and the adolescent hesitations that were to give a style of expression and behaviour to a whole generation of young men. James Dean (Cal) is first seen sitting crouched on a wooden sidewalk, his face concentrated in doubt or disbelief, trying not to watch as the little lady in black passes behind him – the town madam, Kate, later established as Cal's hitherto 'dead' mother. Fretful and awkward he tails her at a distance up the streets and alleys into the dusty wide lanes on the outside of town. He stands under the trees outside her house, scuffing with his feet, hands deep in his pockets, until his suppressed anguish breaks out and he picks up a stone, flinging it across the garden at the house. When the bouncer comes out to him Cal is tentative and half-afraid, not yet ready to fight. He indicates the lady in black watching him through her curtains: 'Would she talk to me?' And when the man chases him off, his defiance is petulant like that of a child. 'You tell her – I hate her.'

Cal rides home on the freight train and picks up the thread of his own life again, lost in the trees and the green Salinas Valley, shadowing his brother Aron and girlfriend Abra as they walk back from school. Abra's whispered remarks to Aron as they see him, 'the prowler', establishes what the audience has begun to feel about this uneasy boy. 'He doesn't like anyone, does he?…He's alone all the time…He's scary…He looks at you, sort of like an animal.' Aron's incomprehension indicates the sexual connotation of that unease.

The lurking presence or threat is even more explicit in the sequence that follows at the father's newly acquired icehouse and store. Cal is established as the outsider, excluded from the natural bonhomie between the father, Aron and Abra. And when Aron and Abra explore the icehouse loft, Cal is hidden up there in the blocks of ice watching them, eavesdropping on their love talk, the blue of his eyes cold and baleful, lost in inarticulate despair as he chips the ice spike at the blocks. Again the suppressed anguish breaks out with the sudden, petulant violence of a child: in a spasm of energy he hooks the blocks of ice out of the loft with the spike, sending them cascading in a wild, wasteful frenzy down the loading chute.

He returns that night over the mountains to the whore-house in Monterey. Communication, and even contact with his father has been lost and he has to reach out

*Cal tails his mother (Jo Van Fleet) the town madame, Kate, through the streets of Monterey (above); outside
'Kate's' brothel, the bouncer chases him off: 'You tell her – I hate her' (below).*

to someone. He slips through the bouncer at the door into the smoke-laden interior of the whore-house bar, and corners the frightened little barmaid. He has to score with her, and quickly. He needs an ally; someone who will tell him about the lady in black and show him where he can find her. The barmaid has seen him being chased away that morning and she goggles at him in admiration: 'You got a nerve, kid…coming back here.' She is carrying a tray of drinks in her hand to serve at one of the tables, but is frozen reluctantly with him at the corner of the bar, hypnotised, as he leans twisted on the counter to keep his face hidden from the bouncer. Bette Treadville creates a perfect miniature study of this girl, frightened to mouth-open distraction by the brutality of her surroundings. Browbeaten and inarticulate she responds now to the gentle intensity of the young intruder. He asks her about the whore-house madam, Kate. Does she treat the girl well? And when she shrugs he asks her with desperation: 'Is there anything nice about her at all?'

The maid shows him where to find Kate, up a long dark corridor away from the bar (Kazan retains the corridor as a strong recurring image throughout the film). Cal pushes open a door, finds his mother sleeping in a chair and drops to his knees in front of her, watching her, examining her, until she awakes to scream for the bouncer. Cal is dragged away back down the corridor, scrabbling at the walls, clinging desperately onto a water-pipe to hold himself with her: *Talk* to me please, mother.'

Later in the film Cal returns, successfully this time, to confront Kate and ask her for a loan. The scene fluctuates nicely between their mutual curiosity, their respective needs for and mistrust of contact and affection, the aloof, suspicious coldness of the mother, the impatience of Cal for the money he is asking. It is Cal's eagerness that dominates the end of that scene. As the mother is writing out the cheque, his whole attention and demeanour is concentrated on that little slip of paper, and he is unable to keep his hands, and even his body, from reaching out for it.

Most of the successful highpoints, both of the film and of Dean's acting, are achieved in Cal's scenes with the women: the barmaid, his mother, and Abra. For these are the relationships in which Dean could use that physical presence to its best advantage. They are also more successfully dramatised than the two supporting male roles of father and brother, in which the characterisations are too obvious: Raymond Massey, stiff and totally predictable; Richard Davalos, the angelic goody-goody with sly tendencies. Aron's weaknesses (as much in the writing as in the acting) are reflected in the dramatic short-comings towards the end of the film, when neither his agonising over the war nor his violent quarrel with Cal, is made sufficiently believable.

It is only Cal's viciousness that makes Aron suddenly real, after their quarrel and after the father's refusal of Cal's money. He takes his brother to the whore-house, leads him up the dark corridor to Kate's room, slips open the door, and pulls him inside: 'Aron, say hello to your mother'; then pushes his brother across the room at her.

At the end of the film, where Cal is reconciled with his now paralysed bed-ridden father, the audience's involvement is again inhibited by a hitherto one-dimensional portrait of the father, once more the fault of the dramatisation more than the acting. It is only the concern of Abra for Cal, and her efforts to make the father respond to him, that bring any kind of reality to a scene that degenerates into whispering mumbo-jumbo.

Cal's love affair with Abra has developed initially through two scenes, the lunch-break in the fields during the lettuce harvest, and the fairground scene after the outbreak of war. Both sequences are situations where Abra, waiting for Aron, is side-tracked by her fascination for the other brother. In the fields she watches the Mexican girl who has been making a play for Cal: 'Girls follow you around, don't they?' Cal is nervous with Abra,

'Talk to me please, mother.'

and his physical unease communicates the sexual threat: he sits cross-legged, eating his lunch; he lies down; he shifts, he stretches, never for a moment still, Dean's body in full expression as she watches him and talks to him.

In the fairground scene Abra observes Cal in laughing disbelief, talking down the soldier who has been trying to pick her up, stealing from the fairground stalls, clowning in the distorting mirrors. They ride the big wheel and sit alone, isolated above the town when the wheel suddenly stops. She is already talking to him more easily and more frankly than she can to Aron, finding in Cal's isolation and loneliness something of her own insecurity, the doubts and desires that Aron cannot understand. When he turns his head to her their need for physical contact is overpowering and the kiss, with its implications of fratricide and incest, is erotic far beyond any scene of more explicit sex (to achieve the discomfort and nervous intensity of that scene, Dean apparently played it with a near to bursting bladder after a day's deliberate abstinence from the lavatory). The kiss on the big wheel, like the kiss with Natalie Wood in *Rebel*, plays the sensuality of movement, Dean turning his head, lips parting minutely towards the girl, but in the end making the girl move to his mouth.

Following the fight that results between the two brothers, Cal, half-drunk and in despair, climbs to the flat roof outside Abra's bedroom to talk with her through the window. But after the eroticism of their preceding sequences it is a disappointing and noncommittal scene, in no way remedied by Cal's head-banging, Brando-style masochism. A different, and by all accounts more effective sequence, was apparently shot either as a screen test, or as an alternative and discarded scene. In it Cal actually climbs through the window into the bedroom and, echoing Brando's performance with Eva Marie Saint's glove in *On the Waterfront*, caresses one of Abra's shoes while she sleeps in her bed.

Cal with the barmaid (Bette Treadville) as he searches for his mother.

That scene on the roof, and an earlier scene in the sheriff's car, were the two occasions in *East of Eden* where Dean's acting was unquestionably mannered with Brando-like gestures and expressions. During the sequence in the car, where the sheriff (Burl Ives) is telling Cal the history of his father's quarrel with the mother, Cal is twisting around, climbing out the window, hanging on the roof, wrapping himself round the door pillars, in an unnecessarily cute exhibition of youthful concern.

Comparisons between Dean and Brando were already rife even before work on the film had started. The two of them (with many others, less well known) were representative of a new realism influencing not only acting but also writing (dialogue) and film production (the use of real locations).

So far as acting was concerned audiences were not used to the conventions of the new style: the half-articulate searching for words (Brando) or rejecting of words (Dean); and the disturbing physical movements, the implied narcissism of 'whole body' acting. Until the arrival of Brando as Stanley Kowalski in *A Streetcar Named Desire* or of Montgomery Clift and Frank Sinatra as Prewitt and Maggio in *From Here to Eternity*, the Hollywood anti-hero had always been expressed through largely extrovert acting – James Cagney, Paul Muni, Humphrey Bogart, or to a slightly more introspective degree, John Garfield. Now for the first time in Hollywood cinema the anti-hero was discarding the polished gesture, timing and delivery. He was behaving instead like a real juvenile delinquent off the city streets, like a drunken soldier on furlough, or a truck driver in a rough diner.

While this realism originated in the socialist background of the fringe theatres of the

Cal anxiously watches his mother write out the cheque for his bean field investment.

1930s, a new liberating influence had been the wartime neo-realism of the new Italian film directors, Roberto Rossellini, Vittorio De Sica, and Luchino Visconti. Actors like Raf Vallone, Anna Magnani, Maria Michi, Emilio Cigoli or Aldo Fabrizi, had adapted their styles to blend with the naturalism of non-professional players in *Rome Open City*, *Shoeshine* and *Paisa*. *Bicycle Thieves* and *La Terra Trema* were made entirely with non-professionals, and De Sica and Visconti had selected observations of natural behaviour that gave audiences (and especially the actors among them) a new access to real emotions and a truer understanding of human nature.

The style of acting that evolved from these influences, and through the so-called 'method' of Strasberg and the Actors Studio, attracted inevitable criticism and abuse. Fred Magdalany described 'Brandoism' in the *Daily Mail*: 'The portrayal of a character not recognisably human, by an actor not recognisably acting.' Brando was dubbed the 'mumble-scratch' actor; Montgomery Clift the 'blank stare perplexed' actor. Old-fashioned professionals, whether actors, directors or technicians, hated the bad delivery, the mumbling, the pauses, the turning away in the middle of the phrase, the jerky and unpredictable interruptions of gestures and scowls. To them the style was a fad and those who acted by it merely copying a fashion. And like Paul Newman after him, Dean was accused of copying Brando.

Natalie Wood, who worked with Dean on *Rebel Without a Cause* and later with Kazan on *Splendour in the Grass*, believes the resemblance had more to do with the director than with either of the two actors: 'Jimmy was often accused of imitating Marlon Brando. The person I think they both possibly were under the influence of was Kazan. Any common mannerisms were Kazan.' Nicholas Ray, Dean's director on *Rebel*, and earlier an assistant

Cal and his mother are drawn together by their mutual curiosity (above); Abra flirts with Cal during the lettuce harvest (below).

The anti-German mob in the fairground.

on Kazan's first picture, attributed these common mannerisms to Kazan's habit of acting out scenes for his players. Dean's own reaction to the rivalry was complicated by an almost fanatical admiration of Brando's acting and life-style. He commented himself at the time: 'It is impossible not to carry around with one the image of so successful an actor.'

Looking back at those early performances of Brando and Dean it is difficult to see the resemblance that was so strongly emphasised by critics at the time. It was six years after the release of *East of Eden* before a retrospective analysis by Dilys Powell in the *Sunday Times* put the Brando-Dean argument into some sort of perspective:

> When *East of Eden* appeared it was fashionable to say that Dean tried to imitate Brando. Well if he tried he certainly didn't succeed, and in the result the only resemblance I can see is in the use of the broken half-masticated phrase. Brando is all power: power sometimes pinioned, or trapped, or degraded, but still power. James Dean was sentenced by physique to stand for defencelessness, and some instinct, far more than the actor's technique, taught him how to suggest, behind the mask of rebelliousness, a different being, shrinking, fragile, not quite fully grown. As long as he stuck to that he had no equal; and looking again at this first film [*East of Eden*] I am astounded by his performance. It is even better than I had thought: more truly anguished, more delicately poised between the awkward sulky scapegoat and the young creature exploding with love. It gives heart and centre to the film, it breathes life into Kazan's melodramatics.

When the *East of Eden* unit moved from location into the studios on 11 June, Brando had started work on his part as Napoleon in the Twentieth Century Fox production, *Desirée*.

Dean had long revered Brando's acting and his uncompromising life-style and he now tried, without great success, to make friends with his idol. He was often seen at the Twentieth Century Studios watching Brando at work. Brando's only recorded comment to him at this time was a disparaging reference to Dean's Brando-style clothes: 'Whyn't wear sumpin' else 'sides last year's suit?' (Since Dean's arrival on the Hollywood scene Brando had given up his jeans and jerkins for clean shirts and slacks.) The columnists, having already labelled Dean the 'poor man's Brando', were quick to accentuate any rivalry between the two young actors, spotlighting Brando's occasional disparaging remarks, and drawing them ultimately into an unnecessary feud. It was one of Dean's wilder fantasies that he would some day challenge Brando to an acting duel to prove conclusively who was the greater.

In an interview two years later, after Dean's death, Brando was asked by Truman Capote whether he had been at all close to Dean: 'No, Dean was never a friend of mine…I hardly knew him. But he had an *idée fixe* about me. Whatever I did he did. He was always trying to get close to me. He used to call up…I'd listen to him talking to the answering service, asking for me, leaving messages. But I never spoke up. I never called him back. When I finally met Dean, it was at a party, where he was throwing himself around, acting the madman. So I spoke to him. I took him aside and asked him didn't he know he was sick? That he needed help…He listened to me. He knew he was sick. I gave him the name of an analyst and he went. And at least his work improved. Towards the end I think he was beginning to find his own way as an actor.'

It was during Dean's work on his third and last film, *Giant*, that Brando's attitude seemed to relax somewhat towards his rival. One of Dean's girlfriends, Maila Nurmi, used to meet both of them around Hollywood at that time and Brando once said to her: 'Tell your friend – that boy you run with – that I think the greatest actors in the world are Paul Muni, Laurence Olivier and James Dean!' Delighted with the compliment Dean returned the message, again through Maila Nurmi: 'You know I think the greatest actors in the world are Paul Muni, Laurence Olivier and Marlon Brando.'

According to Dennis Hopper, Dean met with even greater reluctance when he tried to approach Montgomery Clift: 'Jimmy used to call Monty Clift when he was in New York and say, "I'm a great actor and you're my idol and I need to see you because I need to talk to you and I need to communicate." And Clift would change his phone number. Then after Jimmy was dead Monty Clift saw all three of his films and every time he'd get drunk and cry and cry about the fact he'd denied this young man the opportunity of seeing him and talking to him.'

The columnists were trying hard to invent or accentuate rivalries and vendettas but working even harder to construct a love life for Warner Brothers' new young star, anticipating potential romance each time Dean turned his head in the studio canteen, and faithfully cataloguing Dean's girlfriends in the hope that one of them would survive more than a single evening's date. For those who had known Dean in New York there was nothing strange or new about this endlessly changing parade of female (and male) companions. He would spend evenings with them; joke with them; play the attentive escort; ignore them if they bored him; maybe sleep with a few of them. They would usually last for as long as they made no emotional demands and if such a situation arose, he could be ruthlessly and cruelly dismissive.

The sexing of Hollywood in those mid-1950s was very ritualistic. Stars had to be seen to date, boys with girls, girls with boys – whatever else they might choose to do between the sheets. Studio publicists would take the statutory pictures throughout a romance, up to and including a honeymoon, and supply the captions and stories to content the magazines. Real-life and dangerous affairs were still allowed to be discreet. Dean watched both his

Elia Kazan, Marlon Brando, Julie Harris and James Dean on the Warner lot.

favourite film directors mix business and passion without a word ever being printed by the columnists – Kazan with Julie Harris, Nicholas Ray with Natalie Wood.

It would certainly never have crossed anyone's mind to speculate about Dean's bisexuality. Homosexual Hollywood was largely left to its own devices in an environment far more sheltered than socialist or left-wing Hollywood, where McCarthy's witch-hunt continued to carve its way through friendship and loyalty in an open celebration of betrayal, from which the American soul has never really recovered. Paranoia about 'reds under the bed' seemed to leave the stars' behaviour inside the bed comparatively unscrutinised and the media of those days were more restrained in their invasions of celebrity privacy. While studio publicity machines worked to manicure their heterosexual images, Tab Hunter and Anthony Perkins remained relatively unscathed by rumour and Rock Hudson could openly date with George Nader – even turn up at gay parties in drag (though in the end, speculation in the gossip columns did finally drive Rock Hudson into his brief and token marriage with Phyllis Gates).

During these last fifteen months of his life there was only one girl who succeeded in drawing Dean, however briefly, out of his self-absorption. On the day *East of Eden* transferred into the studios, the actress Pier Angeli, loaned to Warners by MGM, was reporting to an adjoining stage to co-star with Paul Newman in *The Silver Chalice*. It was not long before the young Italian girl was introduced to the notorious 'rebel' star next door and encouraged by the Studio publicists to 'date'. But this 'dating' was altogether different from the stage-managed flirtations so far contrived. The two of them were soon spending their lunch-breaks and evenings together, and only a week after meeting him Pier Angeli was reported as having spent the afternoon of her twenty-first birthday helping Dean brush down his palomino out at the ranch.

At the beginning of July Dean was actually seen, and photographed, in a tuxedo, escorting Pier Angeli to a theatre premiere. But such formality was rare. Most evenings they spent walking, horse-riding, or talking and clowning in the sort of restaurants where Dean was still admitted in his jeans or riding breeches.

The twenty-one-year-old Italian was a world away from the girls Dean had known – soft-spoken, shy, fragile and serious. She had come to Hollywood two years previously, to play the part of the young GI bride in Fred Zinnemann's film *Teresa*. MGM had signed her up with a contract that forbade her to use make-up or to frequent places of public entertainment. Her unspoilt virginal image was to be protected – though virginal innocence was not necessarily genuine. Pier Angeli had had 'affairs' already with Kirk Douglas, John Barrymore and Eddie Fisher. She had now settled permanently in Hollywood, living with her twin sister, film star Marisa Pavan, the two of them supervised and carefully chaperoned by their ambitious mother.

James Dean, with his Quaker mid-west upbringing, had had no experience of possessive, Latin and Catholic mothers. The first time he escorted Pier Angeli home, some hours later than expected, her mother challenged him at the door. This was no time to bring a respectable Italian girl back home. 'When in Rome, do as the Romans do,' Dean told her. 'Welcome to Hollywood.' Not surprisingly maternal pressure was brought on the girl to drop her new admirer. Again it was not a situation with which Dean was familiar: the pressure on Pier Angeli did not consist of commands or prohibitions. The family unit was threatened and the conflict for the girl was not of authority, but of loyalties. She became unhappy, and Dean could not understand how to help her.

East of Eden was by now entering its final two or three weeks of shooting and expectations were already high. The viewing theatre was always packed out for rushes and the publicity office had been told to prepare special treatment for the film and its new young star. No one wanted disappointments, least of all Kazan: 'He got into something with Pier Angeli and got very upset. He had an uncertain relationship with women. He got upset and it was affecting his work, so since I was alone – my wife wasn't there – I told him I'm going to live in the dressing room, I don't want to live in the hotel any more. I got into the dressing room next to him and we both lived in adjoining dressing rooms on the lot... so I kept my eye on him night and day, so we'd be sure to get through the goddam picture.'

The arrangement was more comfortable than it sounds. Although actors were not permitted to 'live in' during filming, each of the larger dressing rooms was equipped with a bathroom and cooking facilities. Kazan persuaded Warners to bend their no-accommodation rules and so far as the work was concerned, this close proximity of actor and director had its advantages. Whenever there were problems with the part they could work on them in the evenings. Kazan recalls difficulties on one particular scene: 'We spent all afternoon and he couldn't do it right, so I got him loaded on red wine that night. He couldn't drink a lot because he was sort of unstable, and liquor would affect him, but I gave him two drinks of wine and he did the scene great.'

Kazan had used a more subtle approach to an acting problem with Raymond Massey. In the evening scene that follows Cal's first violent outburst – pushing the ice-blocks out of the ice store loft – his father makes him read some verses from the Bible. Cal, slumped on an elbow across the table, is already unrepentant about the ice. 'I wanted to see it slide down the chute.' He angers his father still further by punctuating his Bible reading with the verse numbers, and the scene called for a final explosion from the father which Massey could not seem to give. Without telling the religious and rather strait-laced Massey, Kazan gave Dean new lines instead of the Bible verses. They did the next take and Dean whispered his substituted lines: 'Fuck shit God and piss on Jesus.'

Massey, enraged, yelled for Kazan, shouting that he refused to work with the boy any more. The situation was explained and peace restored. But the cameras had kept running and Kazan at last had the reaction he was working for.

They were going to buy a home in Beverly Hills, and honeymoon in Italy. Two months later she married Vic Damone.

Dean's relations with Massey were fairly uneasy throughout the film – as indeed was required by their roles. Massey, the old-fashioned professional, did not approve of Dean's acting theories, and particularly not in his time-wasting exercises and the long meditations that preceded every new scene.

It was during these final weeks that Dean had to face what was probably his most difficult moment in the film, again with Raymond Massey: the scene where Cal's father refuses his son's gift of money. It is the father's birthday, and Cal and Abra have prepared a celebration, decorating the house. The father comes in, surprised and pleased, and Cal gives him the neatly wrapped packet of money. When he sees what it is, the father will not accept it. It is profit made out of speculating on the labour of poor farmers. He rejoices instead in brother Aron's present – the announcement of his engagement to a surprised Abra. Cal is shattered, and attempts to embrace his father in a desperate, whimpering appeal for warmth and affection.

Kazan had been trying the climax of the scene, the attempted embrace, in close-up. But as so often in his acting Dean found his most graphic expression by using the whole of his body: '…He was terribly tense and pent-up. And then when he got loose you felt some little string had been tugged and he went into this jiggle. When he dropped the money from behind his father's back, he went "Ahhhh", and spun around with his arms outstretched – like a weird puppet.'

There again, the scene as finally played was sprung without warning on the unfortunate Raymond Massey. When Dean came crying and embracing him, Massey's horrified reaction was entirely spontaneous and genuine.

'Dean's body was very graphic; it was almost writhing in pain sometimes. He was very twisted, almost like a cripple or a spastic of some kind. He couldn't do anything straight. He even walked like a crab, as if he were cringing all the time.' Most of Kazan's appreciation of James Dean's acting was tempered by his dislike of him as a person, and this personal antipathy often made him, on his own admission, less than kind or patient. 'Directing James Dean was like directing the faithful Lassie. I either lectured him, or terrorised him, flattered him furiously, tapped him on the shoulder, or kicked his backside. He was so instinctive and so stupid in many ways.'

Kazan had never liked Dean from the days he had first come across him at the Actors Studio, and had always compared him unfavourably with Brando. 'Dean was a cripple…inside. He was not like Brando. People compared them, but there was no similarity. He was a far, far sicker kid, and Brando's not sick, he's just troubled.'

Dean was certainly more vulnerable than Brando, both as an actor and as a person and Kazan had never been particularly tolerant or understanding of weakness in others. Interviewed in 1962, Kazan was asked to comment on the James Dean generation: '…The first manifestation was this one of "Pity me, I'm too sensitive for the world. Everyone's wrong except me." It was a fairly universal attitude. That's why James Dean was an idol everywhere. You see all these little boys around the street still looking as, "I'm a homosexual because my mother did this to me", or "I'm neurotic because this happened to me". They should shake this off and go on to solve the problem.'

Richard Davalos knew better than the others the effect of Kazan's directing on Dean's morale: 'Jimmy didn't know how to take hard criticism. He had no acting persona that could soak it up and deal with it and not let it get through to him too personally. It just bewildered him. Then he'd have to sort himself out, before he could sort out what was wrong in the acting.'

It was Julie Harris who understood this vulnerability. Kazan himself said: 'The great one in that picture, the one who helped it come through behind the scenes, was Julie

Shattered by his father's rejection of the money, Cal makes a desperate, whimpering appeal for warmth and affection.

Harris, because she was so kind and tolerant to Dean. He was difficult and I had to be rough with him several times. But she was very kind to him and she supported him.'

Dean himself never commented on his difficulties with Kazan, and his high opinion of Kazan as a director was apparently never in question. He came to accept Kazan's occasional impatience, and worked hard not to provoke it unnecessarily.

East of Eden finished shooting in the second week of August, and Kazan himself recalls the feeling of expectation: 'We began to suspect something outstanding was going to happen with him [Dean] about three-quarters through the picture. You could just see that he was so good. I've never seen anything like it in the movies in my whole life, including Marlon Brando.'

But for all his appreciation of the actor's skill, Kazan's personal feelings towards Dean had, if anything, deteriorated during the last weeks of filming. 'He got kind of spoiled, abusing, throwing his weight around' – one of a good many unsympathetic remarks from the director who had, by his own admission, been manipulating the young man's emotions and vulnerabilities over the previous three months (Kazan's attitude cannot but remind us of his own behaviour in front of the House Un-American Activities Committee – the "Are You Now Or Have You Ever Been" anti-communist inquisition – when to save himself he had given the names of colleagues and friends: Kazan was just as ruthlessly self-centred as his young actor).

Not that one can deny a paranoia in Dean's behaviour at the end of the film. His dressing room home had become a retreat, jealously guarded; he kept a Colt .45 in the wardrobe and his old switchblade in a back pocket. The few times he drank he was violent and abusive; and whenever he went out in the evening without Pier Angeli, he was always surrounded by a crowd of hangers-on.

Once the filming had finished he stayed on in the dressing room, the solitary occupant of the Warners' lot when the gates closed and everyone had gone home at night. He was feeling the not unusual anti-climax that follows the disbanding of a film unit. The crew and the players had dispersed and they had been his family for the duration of the shoot. He now wanted to return to New York, but there was a TV play to work on in Hollywood. Above all there was his fluctuating love affair with Pier Angeli – 'Miss Pizza', as he asked for when he called her on the telephone. 'Mama Pizza' was, as usual, not amused.

This twilight period was brought to an end by Jack Warner himself, the evening he found Dean wandering around the empty studios. They both abused each other, apparently without knowing who the other person was, and when Jack Warner finally identified himself, he gave Dean twelve hours to pack his bags and get out. Dean was furious. He spent that night sabotaging the studio geography, switching round name-boards and uprooting signposts. When he stormed out in the morning he swore he would never return there to work again. Warner Brothers, it seems, maintained a diplomatic silence. They were already negotiating an extension of Dean's contract. Dean took a temporary room in Sherman Oaks, a suburb of Los Angeles, bought himself a new motorcycle, and worked off his anger or anxieties blazing 'wheelies' up and down Sunset Boulevard.

Establishment Hollywood and the all-powerful columnists were unanimous in their verdict: Dean was getting too big for his black leather boots; his anti-social posturing was stardom gone prematurely to his head.

Inevitably, the more he reacted against the publicity machine, the more exposure he was given. He came into the studio canteen one day and found his framed portrait hung on the wall. He tore the portrait down and smashed it on the floor. 'I told them I didn't want this stuff. I told them no pictures on the wall. No pictures of me in any place. Can't they understand? I don't want it.' Next day the incident was faithfully reported, the latest item to join the glowing collection of 'wild boy' anecdotes.

The lady-queen of columnists, Hedda Hopper, was persuaded to do an interview with him in that same studio canteen. She described the meeting some years later in her autobiography, *The Whole Truth and Nothing But.*

> The latest genius sauntered in dressed like a bum and slouched down in silence a table away from mine. He hooked another chair with his toe, dragged it close enough to put his feet up, while he watched me from the corner of his eye. Then he stood up to inspect the framed photographs of Warners' stars that covered the wall by his head. He chose one of them, spat in its eye, wiped off his spittle with a handkerchief, then, like a ravenous hyena, started to gulp the food that had been served him.

Hedda Hopper walked out on the scene and dismissed Dean with a few words in her column next day:

> They've brought out from New York another dirty-shirt-tail actor. If this is the kind of talent they're importing, they can send it right back so far as I'm concerned.

The attitudes adopted by unsympathetic journalists, understandable in the context of Hedda Hopper's abortive interview, were best summarised in a later article, quoting Maurice Zolotov:

> He [James Dean] was surly, ill-tempered, brutal, without any element of kindness, sensitivity, consideration for others, or romantic passion. He was physically dirty. He hated to bathe, have his hair cut, shave, or put on clean clothes. He smelled so rankly that actresses working in close contact with him found him unbearable.

In contrast to this are Natalie Wood's impressions of her first meeting with Dean, when they were cast together in a television show, *I Am a Fool,* shortly after work had finished on *East of Eden*:

> It was a half-hour drama for General Electric Playhouse. Eddie Albert was also in it. It was based on a rather well-known short story – I can't remember the name of the author. All I remember is that it was the story of a man looking back on his youth, so that Jimmy was playing Eddie Albert as a young man and remembering his first love. For me it was the first time I had done a love scene on screen. As for Jimmy, he was unusual for that time in that he arrived at work on a motorcycle looking rumpled – though he was nice and clean. Just rumpled. He didn't comb his hair a lot. He arrived through a garage side entrance and had to jump down into the rehearsal hall, which was really an old building. He had a safety-pin holding his pants together. He was introspective and very shy. The producer, Mort Abrahams, told him to sit with me since we were the young lovers in the piece. But he just grunted, and we'd got half-way through the reading before he did come and sit by me. He was introspective during the read-through and very indirect in his manner towards people. I remember when I went to lunch I noticed him soundlessly following me. We had lunch together every day while we were working. He always had a radio with him and played classical music. At that time he was very much in love with Pier Angeli. But her mother was breaking off their romance because she didn't believe he had the necessary social graces.

The unhappy climax to his love affair with Pier caught Dean off guard and undefended. He had abandoned his hiding-place and opened himself to the girl. He had visions of the future. As far as he was concerned they were two free spirits; their love was private and shared. He had made no allowances for the outside pressures that were troubling the girl.

He told Richard Davalos, 'For better or for worse I'm going to spend the rest of my days with her.' They were going to buy a home in Beverly Hills with a big garden and fill the place with kids. They would honeymoon in Italy, and he was going to see Vesuvius, collect Etruscan vases, and have a private audience with the Pope.

He took Pier Angeli on one of his rare visits to his father and stepmother in Santa Monica. He rang his New York agent, Jane Deacy, and told her he wanted to get married quickly. He even called up his old childhood mentor, the Rev de Weerd in Fairmount, Indiana to announce his intention of converting to the Catholic faith.

He was displaying an unusual lack of reticence, and there was, who knows, an element of desperation in his plans; an awareness or a premonition that this vision of happy tranquillity was somehow doomed.

Shortly before her own death Pier Angeli talked for the first and only time about her love affair with James Dean in the *National Enquirer*:

> We used to go to the California coast and stay there secretly in a cottage on a beach far away from all prying eyes. We'd spend much of our time on the beach, sitting there or fooling around just like college kids. We would talk about ourselves and our problems, about the movies and acting, about life and life after death… We had complete

James Dean with Pier Angeli at the ranch where he kept his palomino..

understanding of each other… Sometimes on the beach we loved each other so much we just wanted to walk together into the sea holding hands because we knew then that we would always be together… We didn't have to be seen together at film premieres or nightclubs. We didn't need to be in the gossip columns or be seen at the big Hollywood parties. We were like kids together and that's the way we both liked it… Sometimes we would just drive along and stop at a hamburger stand for a meal or go to a drive-in movie. It was all so innocent and so emphatic.

Towards the end of September Dean had to leave Hollywood for a television commitment in New York. He spent a last evening with Pier Angeli trying to persuade her to come with him. It seems that the night ended with a quarrel, Dean abrupt and cold, the Italian girl more than ever perplexed and unhappy.

On the day James Dean left Los Angeles, Pier Angeli met Vic Damone at the Warner Brothers Studios. They were old friends and hadn't seen each other for some time. They met again at a party that same evening, and next day Damone visited Pier Angeli's mother. He was well-spoken, Catholic, of Italian origin and most attentive to the Signora. Twenty-four hours later, Dean read of Damone's engagement to Pier Angeli in the New York papers. For some days he refused to believe it. When a Hollywood friend told him it was true, he broke down and cried.

Whether they ever met or spoke together again, no one knows. It was in Dean's character to fight for something so important; but it was equally in his character to shut a hurt away. His friends watched him withdraw, the veil come down, the black moods return, his personal self-confidence evaporate.

The Vic Damone/Pier Angeli wedding took place on 24 November, one of the big social events in Hollywood that year: a church packed with celebrities; thirty-two choirboys dressed in red, white and gold cassocks; Wagner's 'Tannenbaum'; the Mendelssohn 'Wedding March'; and one uninvited guest outside the church on the far side of the street:

> Jim Dean, who used to date Pier, watched the Angeli-Damone wedding a-straddle his motorcycle across from St. Timothy's.   The *Hollywood Reporter*

Apparently Dean rode out of Hollywood after the wedding and disappeared for ten days. Some say that he went back to his uncle's farm in Indiana; others, that he shacked up with actor Nick Adams and that the two of them spent the time building a racing car.

As for the unfortunate Pier Angeli, her marriage ended in 1958 with divorce, and litigation over the custody of her son. A second marriage to Italian band-leader Armando Trovajoli would fail as sadly as the first, and when her acting career faltered she lived for some years in extreme poverty and desperation, relying on the support of family and friends. She died from heart failure or an overdose of drugs in 1971, just as it seemed her career might revive with the offer of a part in *The Godfather*. Shortly before her death she wrote in a letter to a friend: 'I was only in love once in my life, and that was with Jimmy Dean.'

When Dean resurfaced in Hollywood after his disappearance, editing on *East of Eden* was nearing completion. The *Hollywood Reporter* eavesdropped on one of the early private showings.

> Elia Kazan screened *East of Eden* for Tennessee Williams, Christopher Isherwood, and James Dean. A girl sitting near Dean kept sighing 'Who is that wonderful boy?' over each scene – 'til Dean, unable to stand it, fled the projection room, never to return.

A few days later the same paper reported the first trial run with a public audience. 'Sneak preview audience of *East of Eden* went crazy over James Dean.' Kazan himself was there: 'At the first preview of that picture the balcony was full of kids who had never seen him before, and the moment he came on the screen they began to screech, they began to holler and yell, and the balcony was coming down like a waterfall…'

Whatever his private unhappiness, Dean would have enjoyed watching the confused retreat of some old enemies. One change of mind was particularly whole-hearted. Hedda Hopper had been an implacable debunker of his supposed talent, since their abortive meeting in the Warners' canteen. She now turned down her *East of Eden* preview invitation. A friend of hers, Clifton Webb, afterwards telephoned to tell her that he had just seen one of the most extraordinary performances of his life. A private viewing was arranged for Hedda Hopper, who was still, according to her own subsequent confession, determined to be unimpressed. She wrote afterwards: 'I sat spellbound in the projection room. I couldn't remember ever having seen a young man with such power, so many facets of expression, so much sheer invention.'

Dean returned to New York in December, back to his fifth floor apartment in the scruffy old brownstone building on Sixty-eighth Street.

In whatever direction his acting career seemed to be moving, New York still provided his spiritual home, his Manhattan friends, the intellectual stimulus he always craved. And in this particular midwinter the city became a refuge from the emotional confusion of the last few months in Hollywood.

His contract with Warners excluded the possibility of finding work on Broadway, and he was in any event already involved in preliminary discussions with Nick Ray about his

Dancing lessons with Eartha Kitt.

next film commitment. He filled his days instead with a frenzy of study: sitting in on sessions at the Actors Studio; reading; working at his photography; learning and playing his bongo drums through all-night parties; studying new dance techniques with Eartha Kitt, having heard talk at Warners of a forthcoming film on Nijinsky. He joined a rehearsed reading of Sophocles' *The Women of Troy* with Eli Wallach and Anne Jackson, the director Howard Sackler's comment on Dean: 'A very tough guy. He sleeps on razor blades.'

Nick Ray's son, Tony, spent some time with Dean in New York over the holiday. 'I remember over that Christmas, one day he was in despair and no one could get through to him; then the next day we went to see Jacques Tati in *The Big Day* – I think that's what it was called – and Jim was laughing so wildly we had to leave the cinema. He went racing up the aisle hurdling over the ashcans, and when we were out in the street he just became Tati's postman. It was the most brilliant impersonation I've ever seen.'

These were the last weeks Dean ever spent in New York, and indeed the last weeks he spent anywhere in freedom and anonymity. The public release of *East of Eden* was about to make him the most talked-about actor of 1955, and once shooting started on his second film he would be working almost without a break until his death.

Whatever the success of sneak previews in Burbank, Dean was still apprehensive about the public and critical reception for his first leading role. His misgivings were increased by the way Brando and *On the Waterfront* had been acclaimed all over the world. Any film and any actor that followed such triumphs were sure to be an anti-climax.

And yet, almost perversely, he would do little or nothing to help the launching of the film, or the publicity campaign that preceded its release. He made two exceptions – the first when he allowed photographer Dennis Stock to accompany him on a visit he made in February to his uncle and aunt on the Indiana farm, though the trip seems to have been made as much for his own reasons, than in any conscious effort to help publicity. The Dennis Stock photographs, taken in New York and Fairmount, appear in retrospect as some kind of personal statement: as though, with long months of work and two difficult roles in front of him, he wanted to freeze the image for a moment, and state the facts: this is me; this is how I live in my city; this is where I grew up as a kid. A study in narcissism, of course; but naive and truthful with it. He had not felt it necessary, as Brando before him and Bob Dylan after him, to self-dramatise himself or fabricate a romantic or tortured childhood. He was who he was.

Dean's second concession to publicity was an interview granted to Howard Thompson of the *New York Times*, a cool and calculated performance for such an inexperienced interviewee.

ANOTHER DEAN HITS THE BIG LEAGUE

James Dean is the young man who snags the acting limelight in *East of Eden*, which arrived at the Astor last week. Its opening has started a lively controversy over his histrionic kinship with Marlon Brando – and his professional competence. At any rate, 25-year-old Dean, a product of an Indiana farm, Hollywood, television and Broadway, has made an impression and now owns a Warner Brothers contract.

Count his supporting chore in last season's play *The Immoralist* as having threefold significance insofar as the rapid rise is concerned. It netted him the Donaldson and Perry awards, and, indirectly, the attention of director Elia Kazan, then scouting leads for *Eden,* and finally, his flourishing reputation for unvarnished individuality. In a recent chat at his agent's apartment, west of the Yorkville area, Dean gave ample evidence that he was prepared to maintain that individuality.

He sat quietly, awaiting the first query. The slender frame and boyish features suggested a Booth Tarkington hero. The black corduroy shirt and trousers and a penetrating neutrality of expression, magnified by large, steel spectacles, did not. Had he caught *Eden* yet?

'Sure, I saw it,' came the soft abstract reply. His verdict? 'Not bad.

'No, I didn't read the novel. The way I work, I'd much rather justify myself with the adaptation rather than the source. I felt I wouldn't have any trouble – too much, anyway – with this characterisation once we started because I think I understood the part. I knew, too, that if I had any problems over the boy's background, I could straighten it out with Kazan.'

Asked how he happened to turn to acting, Dean hoisted a jodhpur over one knee and lit a cigarette. 'It was an accident, although I've been involved in some kind of theatrical function or other since I was a child – in school, music, athletics.' He rose and began pacing the room. The words came slowly and carefully.

'To me, acting is the most logical way for people's neuroses to manifest themselves, in the great need we all have to express ourselves. To my way of thinking, an actor's course is set even before he's out of the cradle.'

An only child of non-professionals, Dean was raised by an aunt and uncle in Fairmount, Ind. 'My father was a farmer, but he did have this remarkable adeptness with his hands,' he said, flexing his own. 'Whatever abilities I may have, crystallised there in high school, when I was trying to prove something to myself – that I could do it, I suppose. One of my teachers was a frustrated actress. Through her I entered and won a state oratorical dramatic contest, reciting a Dickens piece called "The Madman". What's it about? About this real gone cat,' he chanted, 'who knocks off several people. It also begins with a scream,' he remembered casually. 'I really woke up those judges.

'All these things,' he went on, 'were good discipline and experience for me. After graduation, I went to live with my father in Los Angeles – Mother had died when I was a kid – and just for the hell of it, signed up for a pre-law [sic] course at UCLA. That did call

for a certain knowledge of histrionics. I even joined a fraternity on the campus, but I busted a couple of guys in the nose and got myself kicked out. I wasn't happy in law either.

'Then I tried my luck in pictures, contacted an agent, got some small parts in things like *Has Anybody Seen My Gal?*, a Korean War film, *Fixed Bayonets,* and one TV play.

'I came here at the suggestion of Jimmy Whitmore, a fine actor and a good boy, a real New York boy, who wasn't too happy out at Metro.' For what he learned at the Actors Studio, while edging into prominence on television and his Broadway bow, *See the Jaguar,* Dean pointedly credits director Lee Strasberg, 'an incredible man, a walking encyclopaedia, with fantastic insight'.

Would he compare the stage and screen media? 'As of now, I don't consider myself as specifically belonging to either. The cinema is a very truthful medium because the camera doesn't let you get away with anything. On stage, you can even loaf a little, if you're so inclined. Technique, on the other hand, is more important. My real aim, my real goal, is to achieve what I call camera-functioning on the stage.

'Not that I'm down on Hollywood. Take pictures like *The Ox-Bow Incident,* most of the Lubitsch ones. Gadge (Kazan), of course, is one of the best. Then there's George Stevens, the greatest of them all. I'm supposed to do *Giant* for him. This guy was born with the movies. So real, unassuming. You'll be talking to him, thinking he missed your point, and then – bang! – he has it.'

How did his Warner contract read? 'Nine films over a six-year period.' Story approval? 'Contractually, no – emotionally, yes. They can always suspend me. Money isn't one of my worries, not that I have any.

'Don't get me wrong. I'm not one of the wise ones who try to put Hollywood down. It just happens that I fit to cadence and pace better here as far as living goes. New York is vital, above all, fertile. They're a little harder to find, maybe, but out there in Hollywood, behind all that brick and mortar, there are human beings, just as sensitive to fertility. The problem for this cat – myself – is not to get lost.' Dean's smile spread as far as his lenses.

A selection of Dennis Stock's pictures were to be published in *Life* magazine during the week of the *East of Eden* premiere and the *New York Times* interview a few days later. This apparent change in Dean's attitude encouraged Warners to lay on a reception for the New York critics, where they were to meet the new young star. But Dean was unrepentant and turned up three-and-a-half hours late for this, his first VIP-style press conference. Warner Brothers were not amused.

The public opening of *East of Eden* was now scheduled for a big Times Square 'World Premiere': tickets at fifty dollars each, to include a dinner party at the Sheraton Astor Roof. The proceeds were dedicated, appropriately enough, to the Actors Studio, and the cinema usherettes for the evening included Marilyn Monroe, Marlene Dietrich, and Eva Marie Saint. Short of guarding him with security men, Warners had done everything possible to ensure Dean's attendance: he was told he could come dressed as he liked; that he could leave the dinner party whenever he wished; that he was not expected to perform for the press.

The day before the premiere, Dean rang Jane Deacy: 'I'm sorry, Mom, but you know I can't make this scene. I can't handle it.' Jane Deacy alerted the Warners executives, and frantic efforts were made to contact him. It was too late. Dean had called Jane Deacy from the airport, and was already in an airplane on his way back to Hollywood.

For a while it seemed that Dean's apprehensions about the critics had not been exaggerated. Bosley Crowther in the *New York Times* described him as:

A mass of histrionic gingerbread. He scuffs his feet, he whirls, he pouts, he splutters, he leans against walls, he rolls his eyes, he swallows his words, he ambles slack-kneed – all like Brando used to do. Never have we seen a performer so clearly follow another's style. Mr Kazan should be spanked for permitting him to do such a sophomoric. Whatever there might be of reasonable torment in this youngster is buried beneath the clumsy display.

In the *New York Herald Tribune* William Zinsser drew that similar parallel with Brando, but felt that Dean conveyed a great deal more of his own characterisation:

Everything about Dean suggests the lonely misunderstood nineteen-year-old. Even from a distance you know a lot about him by the way he walks – with his hands in his pockets and his head down, slinking like a dog waiting for a bone. When he talks, he stammers and pauses, uncertain of what he is trying to say. When he listens, he is full of restless energy – he stretches, he rolls on the ground, he chins himself on the porch railing like a small boy impatient of his elders' chatter … occasionally he smiles unaccountably, as if at some dark joke known only to him…

François Truffaut, writing for *Cahiers du Cinema*, recognised the makings of a cult figure.

East of Eden is the first film to give us a bauderlairian hero, fascinated by vice and contrast, loving the family and hating the family at one and the same time. The concern of a film journal must be with James Dean, the freshly plucked 'fleur du mal', James Dean who is the cinema, in the same sense as Lillian Gish, Chaplin, Ingrid Bergman, etc. James Dean has succeeded in giving commercial viability to a film which would otherwise scarcely have qualified, in breathing life into an abstraction, in interesting a vast audience in moral problems treated in an unusual way... His short-sighted stare prevents him from smiling, and the smile drawn from him by dint of patient effort constitutes a victory. His powers of seduction – one has only to hear an audience react when Raymond Massey refuses the money, which is his love – are such that he can kill father and mother on the screen nightly with the full blessing of both art-house and popular audiences. His character in this film is a synthesis of *Les Enfants Terribles* – a solitary heir to the triple heritage of Elizabeth, Paul, and Dareglos.

It was one of the West Coast critics who came nearest to forecasting the extraordinary effect Dean would have on audiences of his own generation. In the *Hollywood Reporter* Jack Moffit defined:

The box office asset of a handsome and dynamic young actor named James Dean. This is the boy who is apt to captivate the typical movie fans whether or not they like tragic stories. He is that rare thing, a young actor who is a great actor, and the troubled eloquence with which he puts over the problems of misunderstood youth may lead to his being accepted by young audiences as a sort of symbol of their generation. He's the only actor I've ever seen who'd be completely right for Romeo... If this film is to reap the profits it deserves no time should be lost in giving him a big fan magazine build-up, not because he is trivial, but because it's the quickest way to rally people to his support.

It seemed the 'people' would not need much rallying. The gala premiere attracted one of the largest ever recorded crowds in Times Square, and from that evening on, the queues outside the Astor Cinema were stretching round the block, day and night. The same story was repeated wherever the film was released, all over the United States and Canada, in London, Paris, Rome and Warsaw.

Having resisted so much of the Hollywood ballyhoo, Dean himself was quite unprepared for such a spectacular popular reaction. Four days after the film opened in Los Angeles the *Hollywood Reporter* noted:

Jimmy Dean, bespectacled and blue-jeaned, driving down the Hollywood Boulevard, gaping at the *East of Eden* waiting lines – a nightly routine with the flabbergasted young star.

It was the only one of his three films Dean ever saw released. He would not survive to taste success again.

6. Rebel Without a Cause

Whatever's inside me making me what I am,
it's like film. Film only works in the dark.
Tear it all open and let in the light and you
kill it.

James Dean

EAST OF EDEN had expressed the timeless conflict between a father's rigidity and an
adolescent's search for love or understanding; and a generation of young people had
begun to identify instinctively with the pain and bewilderment of James Dean's Cal.
In his next film identification became more specific. Jim Stark was directly representative
of that generation's frustration and of their implied, if barely articulate, rejection of the
materialist values with which they had been brought up.

Rebel Without a Cause originated in a book of that title written by Dr Robert Lindner at
the end of the Second World War: the factual case-history of a teenage psychopath. The
film rights of the book had been bought by Warner Brothers in 1946, and the young, as yet
untried Marlon Brando had been signed up for the lead. But the studio executives were
doubtful about the commercial viability of a film on teenagers. The script failed to
convince them, and the project was dropped.

By the time Nicholas Ray picked the property off the Warners' shelves seven years
later, the context of adolescent drama had radically changed: Luis Buñuel had won the
1951 Cannes Film Festival with *Los Olvidados*, his film on teenage delinquency in the
shanty town suburbs of Mexico City; and J. D. Salinger had won critical and public
acclaim for his novel *Catcher in the Rye*, the story of a rebellious teenager. Television
drama then adopted the themes of adolescent violence or soul-searching, and Hollywood
had finally ventured forth with *The Wild One* and *Blackboard Jungle*, both of which were
well into profit by the time Warners gave Nick Ray a low budget go-ahead on *Rebel
Without a Cause*.

Ray had moved into a Warners' office on 27 September 1954, to start work on
the script. He discarded the old studio scenario, and let the project develop almost
as an improvisation from his own research and from his collaborations with three
writers and with his team of actors. The result was a film recognised by cinéastes
and critics all over the world as a cinema classic of youth in rebellion, worthy of
comparison with its precursors, *Zero de Conduite* and *Los Olvidados,* and
influencing in its own turn François Truffaut's *Quatre Cents Coups* and Lindsay
Anderson's *If....*

Nicholas Ray had come to drama, like Elia Kazan, through the politically and socially conscious fringe theatres of the 1930s: the Group Theatre, the Federal Theatre, the Theatre of Action, the League of Workers Theatre. He had acted in Kazan's stage-directing debut, *The Young Go First* (1936), and after a period with John Houseman on CBS radio and on war propaganda broadcasts, he had worked as assistant on Kazan's film-directing debut, *A Tree Grows in Brooklyn* (1944). In 1945 he teamed up with Houseman again to direct a Broadway musical, *Lute Song*, and in 1946 had started work in CBS Television. It was the success of one of his CBS thrillers, *Sorry Wrong Number*, that brought him to Hollywood movies initially with RKO. His films were always, somewhere, concerned with the parallel themes of violence and the outsider: the deprived adolescent drifting into crime (*Knock on Any Door*); the hard-drinking, aggressive Hollywood writer accused of a murder (Humphrey Bogart, *In a Lonely Place*); the rodeo nomad intruding into the quiet ranch family (Robert Mitchum, Susan Hayward, and Arthur Kennedy, *The Lusty Men*); and the then recent success of Sterling Hayden and Joan Crawford as itinerant cowboy and tough lady bar-owner in *Johnny Guitar*.

In *Rebel* Ray would build the outlines of his story round similar themes, freeing himself stage by stage from the interference of the Warners' front office, and their cosy 'family entertainment' liberalism. He had wanted his old friend Clifford Odets to write the script; Warners instead gave him Leon Uris, who had just completed his own adaptation for them on *Battle Cry*. Ray and Uris parted company after the preliminary research, and Ray was in the early stages of collaboration with Irving Shulman when he first approached Dean about the film: 'I had seen *East of Eden,* had met Jimmy and knew he was the ideal actor for Jim Stark. It was still far from certain, although he was interested in the project, that he would play the part. One side of the difficulty was personal. Since beginning to know him a little, I had realised that for a successful collaboration he needed a special kind of climate. He needed reassurance, tolerance, understanding. An important way of creating this climate was to involve him at every stage in the development of the picture. Accordingly he met Shulman one afternoon at my home.'

Shulman was a sports car addict and Nick Ray had high hopes that the two of them would hit it off together. 'The result was disappointing. After a brief spurt, the talk of cars dwindled away to nothing. Suspiciously, rather menacingly, as happened when rapport was not forthcoming at a first encounter, Jimmy withdrew.'

This meeting took place sometime in December 1954, soon after Pier Angeli's marriage to Vic Damone. Dean was still in his one-room pad in Sherman Oaks, moody and dispirited. It could have been a good time to involve him in a new project, but he probably needed something more concrete and substantial than this sketch of an idea and Ray's enthusiasm.

Ray was himself doubtful whether Warners would let him cast their new gilt-edged star in a low budget, downbeat, black and white picture. The success of the sneak previews of *East of Eden* confirmed his fears. He would need a very firm commitment from Dean to persuade the studio to cast him in *Rebel*.

When Dean took off for New York that month Ray followed a few days later with what existed of Shulman's script, some thirty pages. At least the main areas were now defined: the middle-class background; the 'Romeo and Juliet' relationship in the centre of the story; the scene in the planetarium; and the chicken-run sequence.

Ray spent as much time as possible with Dean while he was in New York. They used to eat together every evening, and then go on to parties or movies. Rather than show Dean the thirty pages of script, Ray talked through the ideas, embroidering and developing them as Dean added his own comments.

For two people who were to get on so well together they certainly took their time

Jimmy Dean with Nick Ray.

making up their minds about each other. Perhaps the collision of two intensities made immediate communication more difficult, or perhaps Dean was genuinely hesitant about a project still in embryo. Ray was quite sure about Dean's suitability for the part, and concerned only with widening his knowledge of Dean as a person: 'The drama of his life, I thought, after seeing him in New York, was the drama of desiring to belong, and fearing to belong (so was Jim Stark's). It was a conflict of violent eagerness and mistrust created very young… The intensity of his desires, his fears, could make the search at times arrogant, egocentric; but behind it was a desperate vulnerability that one was moved, even frightened.'

The evening before Ray returned to Hollywood the two of them were having supper together, Dean still apparently uncommitted to the film. As Ray remembers, he seemed distracted that night, and finally interrupted talk on the script to reveal his particular and rather personal problem.

'"I got crabs," he said. "What do I do?"

'I took him to a drug store to get something for it, and we finally parted in the street outside. He thanked me for my help, smiled, then said: "I want to do your film. But don't let them [Warners] know about it."

'I said I was glad. Then we shook hands on it.'

It was Jean Deacy who now intervened to let Warners know how keen her client was to play the Jim Stark role, and Warners finally announced on 4 January 1955 that Dean had definitely been cast in *Rebel*.

It was just as well that George Stevens was still indecisive over the casting for *Giant*. If Dean had been confirmed for the part of Jett Rink, it is doubtful if *Rebel* would ever have got underway. As events turned out, *Giant*, originally scheduled to begin in March, was postponed two months to give Elizabeth Taylor time to deliver and recover from her baby, and the postponement allowed Dean just enough time to work on both films.

On 18 January Dean arrived in Hollywood to rehearse and film a television play, and whenever he had free time over the next few days he attended script meetings with Ray and Stewart Stern, the young writer who had replaced Shulman. Shulman had left the project after Christmas, following various disagreements with Ray, and Dean's friend, Len Rosenman, had introduced Ray to Stewart Stern. It was the chemistry of Ray, Stern and Dean that now defined the final structure of the script. Ray knew that the characterisation was schematic and one-dimensional, nothing much more than text-book case-histories. He wanted Dean to find the flesh and blood of Jim Stark, out on the streets, and inside his own emotional experiences.

The television play Dean starred in that January was a 'Schlitz Playhouse' drama, *The Unlighted Road*. He played the part of a hitch-hiker who is offered a job in a roadhouse, and becomes involved in a hi-jack conspiracy. The criminals try to pin a murder on him to keep him from talking, but stricken with conscience he confesses all to the police, only to find he has been innocent of the murder all along. The play was telecast on the CBS network in May 1955, and repeated about twice a year, until the print was damaged or destroyed in the 1960s. Apart from interviews and one road safety advert, this was to be Dean's last television appearance.

Dean returned to New York when the play was finished, back to his dancing lessons with Eartha Kitt, and his collaboration with Dennis Stock over the photographic essay commissioned by *Life* magazine. The two of them had made their visit to Fairmount to complete the series of pictures, and though Dean was not to know it, this was another final appearance. Dennis Stock's pictures record his farewell to Indiana and the farm, and appropriately enough include the shots of Dean's lugubrious clowning in the coffins at the back of Wilmur Hunt's village store in Fairmount.

If Dean had premonitions about mortality they could well have been provoked by the peculiar chronology of two events during his week of television work in Hollywood that January. He had met Marlon Brando at a party in Ella Logan's house, and, apparently at the instigation of Ella, Brando had taken Dean aside and lectured him on the perils of motorcycling. Dean had shrugged the advice aside, but a couple of days later took a bad fall on the bike – one of the Hollywood dailies reported cryptically, 'James Dean's bike threw him and bruised his left leg.'

When he came back to Hollywood in early March, fleeing from the *East of Eden* premiere in New York, he declared his intention of selling the bike and buying himself a Porsche sports car. If his friends breathed sighs of relief, their hopes were premature. The Porsche arrived, but somehow the motorbike was never sold, and later the same month Dean borrowed a mechanic from the agent where he had bought the car, and entered himself and the Porsche in two local race meetings at Pacific Palisades and Pasadena. Preparations for *Rebel* were now well advanced and Nick Ray must have viewed his actor's new passion with much apprehension. But he made no attempt to interfere, either then, or later during shooting. It was not until Dean started work on *Giant* that he was obliged by contract to suspend his racing activities.

Hollywood journalists dismissed his motor racing pretensions as nothing more than a publicity gimmick, and his appearance on the circuits was viewed in much the same light by the racing fraternity. Dean quickly proved them wrong, winning his races at Palisades and Pasadena, and entering a more prestigious two-day meeting at Palm Springs. On the Saturday he won the preliminary race, and qualified for the senior race on Sunday. He led that senior race for two-thirds of the distance before being overtaken by a more

In his first Porsche at a race meeting.

experienced driver, Ken Miles. Dean drove the last third of the race trying to regain his lead but finished a hundred yards or so behind. Instead of being content with what was still a remarkable achievement, he was found by his friends after the race 'dancing with rage' beside his car. Nick Adams and the mechanic, Rolf Weutherich, had to drag him away to calm him down for the prize-giving: 'He was trembling like a dead leaf, and on the verge of nervous collapse.'

Ken Miles had two revealing comments to make about Dean's driving after the event: that Dean took insane risks with his own life; but that he would never make it to the top in motor racing because he demonstrated too much concern for the safety of other drivers.

Dean managed three more race meetings before Warners clamped down on him: at Bakerfield, Palm Springs, and Santa Barbara. He totalled six outright victories from his five meetings, and in a few weeks of driving had graduated from the film star dilettante to becoming an accepted and respected member of the racing community. When he blew up his engine at Santa Barbara another competitor paid him the compliment of offering him his spare car for the next race.

Apart from the trips to these motor race meetings out of town, Dean cut himself off from friends and colleagues during the three weeks that preceded filming on *Rebel*. Since his return from New York he had been living a kind of Jekyll and Hyde existence. People would see him occasionally, late at night or in the early morning, wandering like some forlorn hoodlum in dirty clothes, ill-shaven, and often drunk or 'high' on 'bennies' or 'grass'. Bill Bast later wrote in his biography of Dean:

> Perhaps the mental unrest of the characters in the story (*RebelWithout a Cause*) made him want to re-experience the feeling of being lost, unwanted, and different from the norm. But then I began to feel that, this time, it was not so much a matter of study and research as it was a definite and strong feeling he had that he, too, belonged partly to that portion of humanity that is lost, alone, confused.
>
> He had once said to Ella Logan, 'I like you, Ella. You're good. But you know, I like bad people too. I guess that's because I want to know what makes them bad.'

This self-examination, whether clinically or professionally motivated, corresponded with the only period of his life when he was in contact with a psychiatrist. According to contemporary gossip columns, he was seeing Brando's psychiatrist (presumably Dr Mittelman) during that March, though no one seems to know how often they met, nor how involved Dean ever became with analysis. But from the little Dean ever mentioned to his friends on the subject, it appeared that he rejected the experience. 'It's a toss off,' he told Nick Adams, 'they say for me to love my father. I could have told them that fifteen years ago.'

More probably the experience frightened him, in the same way Lee Strasberg's searching and critical analysis had frightened him in the Actors Studio. After his first experience with Strasberg, he had never again performed in front of him. It was likely now that after one or two meetings with the psychiatrist, he would feel vulnerable to the intrusion, and chose not to go on with it: 'Whatever's inside me making me what I am, it's like film. Film only works in the dark. Tear it all open and let in the light and you kill it.'

If Dean was looking for therapy he probably found it easier on the race track. But if he was looking instead for the heart and soul of his rebel, Jim Stark, Dr Mittelman might well have helped expose a layer of Dean's childhood to supply the necessary link.

Once again the emotional centre of Dean's role involved a relationship between father and son, this time the weak father, harried, hen-pecked and castrated, who fails to stand up to

Resting before the race.

Nick Ray rehearsing Dean.

Jim Stark's first day at Dawson High.

the women who run the house, and fails equally to give moral support or help to his son.

The psychological framework is so directly stated as to verge on the cliché:

'You're-tearing-me-apart!' Jim shouts in despair at his parents and grandmother, bickering and contradicting each other over his head. 'You say one thing, he says another, and everyone changes back again.'

It is the force of despair and anger in Dean's performance that gives the lines credibility: the suppressed violence of his emotions always near to flashpoint; the tired, premature wisdom of an adolescent who has already seen and understood so much:

'How can a guy grow up in a circus like that?'

The drama is contained largely within the events of one day – Jim Stark's first day at a new school, Dawson High. The family has just moved into town, the motive behind the move being the trouble Jim has been in at their previous home. In the introductory scene, Jim is already in trouble again, being bailed out of juvenile hall late at night by his parents, drunk and violent. At school next day the only friends he finds are the equally troubled kids he has met in juvenile hall: the school loner, Plato (Sal Mineo), and Jim's next-door neighbour, Judy (Natalie Wood). Again the psychological backgrounds are of textbook simplicity: Plato is the debris of a broken home; Judy has been emotionally rejected by her father. She is also the girlfriend of the school gang-leader, Buzz (Cory Allen). Inevitably Jim and Buzz clash, first in a knife fight, then at a 'chicken-run' – two stolen cars driven fast to the edge of a cliff, the first driver to bail out before the edge being 'chicken'. The 'chicken-run' ends in disaster, Buzz is killed, and Jim is left alone with Plato to comfort Judy. Jim's instinct is to come clean and tell the police what has happened, but his parents want to avoid trouble (his mother threatens to move house again) and the other gang members are scared. Jim, Plato and Judy hide up in a deserted mansion on the outside of town, momentarily happy. But the story ends tragically when the gang finds them. Plato's fears and sense of isolation drive him to violence. Jim tries to shield him, but, in a misunderstanding with trigger-happy cops, Plato is shot and killed.

Juvenile Hall. Jim Stark offers Plato (Sal Mineo) his jacket.

Rebel Without a Cause 'rolled' at the Warners' studios on 28 March 1955 and was immediately in trouble with jittery executives in the front office. The shadow of HUAC (House UnAmerican Activities Committee) still frightened Hollywood. Only a few months previously MGM had balked at the theme of juvenile delinquency in Richard Brooks' film *Blackboard Jungle*. They told Brooks to insert a scene where an authoritative character is given patriotic lines:

> 'You think we have trouble here? You ought to see the juvenile delinquency in Russia.'

Brooks refused to insert any such inane lines, and MGM instead planned a public apologia suggesting that the events in the story could not really happen in the United States of America (on the very day the film opened in New York a school teacher was stabbed and thrown off a roof). Needless to say when the film became a box-office success the apologia was forgotten.

Warners were now having similar doubts about *Rebel*, and in particular about the downbeat ending, and the death of Plato at the hands of the police. Ten days into shooting they were ready to cancel the film, but when Nick Ray threatened to take it elsewhere Warners decided to look at the material already shot and the strength of the drama and the quality of the two main performers, James Dean and Natalie Wood, persuaded them to change their minds. A few days later they told Ray to scrap the material he had already shot and they raised his budget to enable him to shoot the film in colour.

This false start, and the congested schedule that followed, could have undermined the good rapport Ray had built up with his cast. But the feeling of commitment was so strong that no one made any complaints.

Left to right: Nick Ray, James Dean, Sal Mineo, and Natalie Wood.

Ray had achieved the same sense of involvement with the rest of the cast that he had already established with Dean. The script was under continual adaptation, and open to suggestions from all of them. Not surprisingly one of the strong points of the film is the high quality of acting in the supporting roles, in particular Jim Backus' performance as the father, giving substance and dimension to what was, in the script, little more than a caricature of a middle-aged hen-pecked man. It was important to the film that the audience felt the son's ambivalence towards the father, the affection that tempered and tortured Jim's contempt.

Whereas the mother (Ann Doran) had been predictable studio casting, Backus was an unusual choice of Ray's, being more identified as an actor with comedy and with his famous voice on the 'Mr Magoo' cartoons (parodied by Dean in *Rebel* during the sequence round the empty swimming pool at the deserted mansion). Backus was ideally suited to the undertone of comedy in the role: the timing of his fumbling attempts to impose himself on the family scene; the eager-to-be-friends, mournful, half-formed movements of a flaccid well-intentioned face in the scene where Jim finds him, dressed up in an apron, fussing over a spilt tray at the top of the stairs.

For Natalie Wood the film was a coming of age: her first adult or near-adult role in the cinema after a long career as a child and juvenile star (*Rebel* was her twentieth feature film). Dean was lucky with his leading ladies. Julie Harris' performance in *East of Eden* had been delicately and perfectly poised between the childhood friendship of her relationship with Richard Davalos and the sensual recognition provoked by Dean. Now in *Rebel* Natalie Wood made real the desperation of the girl working so hard for love. Handicapped by the brevity of the scenes with her father and the resulting shorthand simplicity of their dialogue, she still convinces with the pained outrage of her rejected affection and the

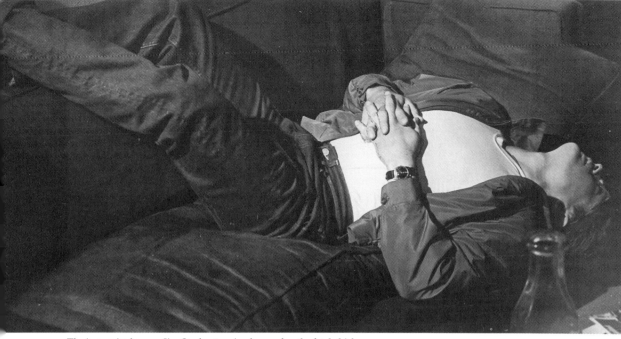

The improvised scene. Jim Stark returning home after the fatal chicken-run.

subsequent yearning for physical warmth in her relationship with Jim. There again reality is made difficult by the time-scale in the script. Jim and Judy have to fall in love during one night, and against the dramatic background of the death of her former boyfriend.

Audacity and simplicity, one could say of the dramatisation in *Rebel*; others would call it an overwrought melodrama. Ray was unafraid of the obvious, and untroubled by the cliché. If he makes them ultimately convincing it is through the reality of detail, and the truth of the image and the performance.

Dean had already been involved with Ray and Stern during the development of the script. He was now given the freedom and responsibility of total collaboration in the performance and characterisation of his role. His work on *Rebel* was the most exacting, the most satisfying and arguably the most successful of his acting career; the achievement, one feels, for which he would have chosen to be remembered.

Kazan had kept a tight rein on Dean throughout *East of Eden*. As in all his films the mood and theme that triumph are his own, and predetermined. Through him the material or content control absolutely. He advised Nick Ray to keep that same tight rein. But Ray, instead, was temperamentally the anarchist. Where he sees life or pertinent truth he stretches the material, and the audience's imagination, to embrace it. In terms of good drama he lives dangerously; the timing and nuance have to be perfect. This was exactly the 'tightrope' atmosphere of Dean's own acting style. The French critic Georges Beaume said of him:

> He acts like a gypsy playing the top string of the violin – a quarter-tone higher, a fraction louder, and it would set the teeth on edge. That judgement is half the pleasure. And James Dean knows very well how far it is possible to go.

In practical terms what Dean found, or rediscovered, with Ray was acting space. He used the term himself: 'When an actor plays a scene exactly the way a director orders, it isn't acting. It's following instructions. Anyone with the physical qualifications can do that. So the director's task is just that, to direct, to point the way. Then the actor must take over. And he must be allowed the space, the freedom to expose himself in the role. Without that space an actor is no more than an unthinking robot with a chestful of push buttons.'

Nick Ray would later cite Dean as the most stimulating actor he had ever worked with, because of the freedom to improvise that they gave to one another. Improvisation led to the timing and expression of the wink Jim gives to Judy at the end of the scene where he drops her outside her home after the death of Buzz – the one gesture that exactly defined their mutual sympathy in that moment, and the only gesture that could make plausible the 'entente' they establish so soon after the death of her boyfriend.

It was improvisation that provided the key to a whole scene through which neither Ray nor Dean could see a way: the moment Jim Stark returns home to a confrontation with his parents after the chicken-run.

The two of them worked it out in improvisation at Ray's home one night: Nick Ray playing the father, sitting himself down with his back to Dean, in front of a blank TV screen so he could watch the reflection of Dean's movements. The living-room communicated directly with the kitchen and he saw Dean entering the house, working himself into the scene, noticing the father asleep in front of the TV, taking a bottle of milk from the fridge, drinking, rolling the cold bottle around his forehead; then Dean's awkward, physical contortion as he lays himself down on the sofa, staring at the ceiling, the silence between him and the sleeping father suggesting some secret, shared communication between them.

Ray called up his art director and had him redesign the set to correspond with his own living-room. Dean played the scene on film exactly as they had improvised it that evening and Nick Ray developed the invention, creating a superb moment of comedy and truth in the 180-degree camera pan when Dean, lying on the sofa, sees his mother appear, sweeping downstairs – upside down from where he is watching her and tilting as he sits up to meet her: the mindless intrusion into that moment of silence between the son and his sleeping father.

Jim Stark's subsequent and violent reaction to his father's further failure to stand up to the mother had Dean grabbing Jim Backus by the lapels of his dressing-gown, lifting him off his feet and hurling him across the room. Both Backus and Ann Doran afterwards recalled the real terror of that moment when the older actor might have fallen and badly injured himself. Instead, Dean, with his phenomenal physical strength and awareness had the older and heavier man in complete control throughout the movement, guiding the fall so that Backus was almost nursed to the ground.

The opening shot of the film was another image largely improvised by Dean. The credits sequence was meant to open with a 'gang rumble': a middle-aged man returning home with presents for his family, beaten up and chased off by Buzz and his henchmen. The man drops a toy, a clockwork monkey, and Dean enters the scene drunk and staggering to pick up the monkey as police sirens approach on soundtrack. When Warners saw it completed they vetoed the violence of that sequence. Ray was left with the single shot of Dean entering scene, lurching down the street, lying down to look at the monkey, wrapping it with scrap-paper against the cold and curling up with it, cheek to cheek, squeezing his body protectively around it. The effect of that single shot was so strong that Ray decided not to reshoot. The monkey is there in the gutter unexplained and the opening shot is concerned with the expression of character and mood, rather than defining the theme of violent juvenile delinquency. But although the image is strong the shot fails to

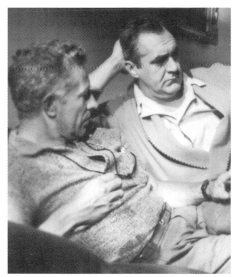

Rehearsing the confrontation between Jim and his parents (Jim Backus and Ann Doran) after Buzz's death.

The opening sequence: the young rebel hero searching for love and understanding.

Jim Stark and the juvenile officer (Edward Platt).

work. Dean is being too cute; and the action never overcomes the initial artificiality of Dean lying down in perfect juxtaposition to the camera. In the absence of the preceding gang rumble the scene needed two shots: a long-shot, as in the still, where the action is only vaguely discernible; and the explanatory close-shot at the end, as the sirens approach.

The concentration of the drama into a time-scale of thirty hours called for a high degree of acting control in the continuity of character and in the transitions of mood. They are achieved so well that, by the end, one is probably less conscious of the time-scale than Ray in fact intended.

Jim's day starts in high hope and expectation: forgiveness for the night's unpleasantness in juvenile hall; and anticipation of new friends during his first day at Dawson High. And up until the lecture at the planetarium the good things still could happen. It is the lecturer's voice that introduces the inevitability of doom and destruction, while Dean, sitting behind Buzz and the gang, is trying to raise a laugh and win the gang's recognition. The lecturer indicates Taurus the Bull on his star-spangled ceiling, and Jim Stark moos loudly from his seat.

BUZZ: Moo. That's real cute.

GOON (Dennis Hopper): Hey – he's real tough.

CRUNCH (Frank Mazzola): I bet he fights with cows.

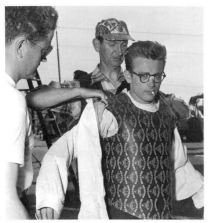

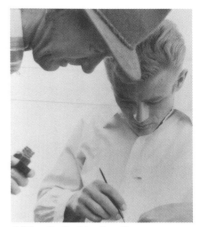

Being fitted with a chest protector.

A brief chat between takes with Nick Ray.

Adding the final touches: the blood-stained shirt.

BUZZ: Moo.

The lecturer briefly silences them all, the weak and the strong alike, with his vision of the earth's death.

LECTURER: We will disappear into the space from which we came, destroyed as we began, in a burst of gas and fire… [loud sound-effects]…The heavens are still and cold once more. In all the complexity of our universe and the galaxies beyond, the earth will not be missed. Through the infinite reaches of space, the problems of man seem trivial and naive indeed. And man existing alone seems an episode of little consequence.

Outside on the planetarium terrace Jim's mood of bouncing hope is literally deflated. Buzz sticks his switch-blade into one of Jim's flashy white-wall car tyres and, sagging with the unavoidability of it all, Jim levers himself off the wall where he is sitting and walks wearily to confront him.

JIM: You know something? You read too many comic books.

BUZZ: Hey! He's real abstract…

Jim tries to avoid the trouble the gang is looking for, and is dubbed 'chicken'. And that for him is the trigger insult. The knife fight that follows is the first violent climax in the film, and, apart from the final confrontation with the cops, the only scene where Jim Stark 'blows his cool'. His sudden anger and his hesitant jerky attempts to control and refuse the fight make suddenly real all the psychotic unease suggested in the juvenile hall the night before. Get it out of yourself, the juvenile officer had told him; and Jim had kicked and punched at the heavy wooden desk until his fury had ebbed away. Now, face to face with Buzz with one of the gang's switch-blades in his hand, we recognise the delinquent who could, after all, kill or maim.

Dean insisted on playing the fight shots for real, to the consternation of the crew and production team. The resulting tension did a lot to heighten the dramatic intensity of the scene – as played by Cory Allen it took on the quality of a dance, a mime of the bullfight, with Buzz playing the tiptoe, hands-high teasing of the banderillero:

The knife fight.

Awaiting the start of the chicken-run (above); Jim and the gang after Buzz has over-run the cliff and killed himself (below).

'What are you waiting for, toreador?'

By contrast the 'chicken-run' sequence was a director's piece, the only acting 'moment' in the first half of the scene being the recognition of friendship between Buzz and Jim as they share a cigarette at the cliff-edge before the run. 'You know something,' Buzz says, 'I like you.' And they walk away to their respective cars while Judy sets up the runway for the contest. Their sympathy has made the 'chicken-run' superfluous, and yet the ritual must proceed.

When Buzz has over-run the cliff and killed himself, Jim, Judy and Plato are left alone, grouped for the first time as a unit. Jim holds out a hand to Judy, not looking at her but drawing her away from the cliff edge where her boyfriend is burning in his car. It is another tightrope moment of acting, but this time a transition that does not quite succeed: the implications are too many, and the gesture itself is too deliberate, drawn-out a moment too long.

Later, after their respective conflicts with parents, Jim and Judy meet outside his garage and talk for the first time about themselves. The scene, with Judy sitting on a wall, and Jim moving restlessly around her, is reminiscent of the picnic scene between Cal and Abra in *East of Eden*. There is Dean's same uneasy animal presence, the same recognition of mutual attraction, the same physical reticence – a near kiss, a near embrace – to create sexual tension.

It is this sexual expectancy that brings menace to the scene in the deserted mansion, while Jim and Judy meet up again with Plato. They are all three of them fugitives, from their families, from the police, from the gang. Yet the triangle of loyalties suggests that the final destruction will come from within themselves, and that Plato, vulnerable and lost, with the gun in his jacket pocket, will be the victim of implied betrayal.

The mood and magic of that empty mansion are shattered by the arrival of Crunch and Goon. Indiscriminate violence is rampant again in Dennis Hopper's mad eyes and foxy, giggling laugh. Plato is trapped by them while Jim and Judy are alone upstairs. He has been deserted, and his gun is the only security left to him. He shoots and wounds Crunch and when the police arrive on the scene, he runs away through the woods to take refuge in the empty planetarium, the lecturer's temple of doom. Jim and Judy follow him into the planetarium and Jim talks Plato into giving him the gun long enough to empty the magazine, another well intentioned betrayal. As in the opening scene at the juvenile hall, he offers Plato his red windcheater to keep him warm. Plato shivers.

The police have ringed the building, an in-turned circle of blazing headlamps and spotlights. Jim leads Plato out, but the light scares Plato, he makes a run for it, and one of the cops shoots him dead. Jim is screaming, hands outstretched: 'I-got-the-bullets!' The spotlights go out. The debris is cleared. The dawn has come. Jim crawls and whimpers like an animal or a child, dragging himself round Plato's body, pulling up the zipper on the red windcheater. His father helps him away, draping him with his own coat. Jim draws his parents to him. Nick Ray is about to get away with reconciliation and Warners with their happy ending. 'Mum, Dad, this is Judy. She's my friend.' The reconciliation is awful. Jim Stark's anger only marginally survives in that he has taken control of the situation. It is he in effect who leads his family and his girl away. He dominates, as James Dean has dominated throughout the film.

A high-shot closes the picture: a man with a briefcase is crossing the lawn towards the planetarium: a forensic expert? The lecturer arriving for another doomsday? Nick Ray himself signing off his movie?

Dean said later he could never again take so much out of himself as he had done on *Rebel*. He felt drained and exhausted, but on this occasion had no time to slip away into the depression and isolation that so often followed his periods of intensive work. Shooting on *Giant* had already begun, and, six hours after completing post-dubbing on *Rebel,* he was on

The deserted mansion: rehearsing with Nick Ray (above); the three fugitives momentarily become the family they yearn for (below).

Quintessential 'teen angels' James Dean and Natalie Wood as Jim and Judy.

his way to begin work in Texas.

Unfortunately he was not to find there the strong creative structure that Nick Ray had built around him during *Rebel*. That partnership had been unique for both of them, a level of communication and creativity that had projected to and dominated everyone who worked on the picture. It gave Dean the maturity he had never shown on any previous occasion. On *East of Eden* he had been very dependent on the kindness and sympathy of others, notably of Julie Harris. Working on *Rebel* he had himself become the elder statesman or master craftsman.

'He was so inspiring, always so patient and kind,' recalls Natalie Wood. 'He didn't act as though he were a star at all. We all gave each other suggestions and he was very critical of himself, never satisfied with his work, and worried about how every scene would turn out. He was so great when he played a scene, he had the ability to make everyone else look great too. He used to come on the set and watch the scenes even when he wasn't in them. He was that interested in the whole picture and not just in his own part.'

'Rehearsing with him kept us all on our toes,' Sal Mineo said. 'Without warning he'd throw in different lines and improvise through scenes. I hadn't seen the rushes and frankly, from what I'd seen of Jimmy on the set, I didn't know what the fuss was about. I didn't think he was very good. Then I saw the screening, and you know, he was great. He was sitting just behind me in the cinema and half-a-dozen times, when he was really terrific, I turned round to look at him. He was giving that grin of his, and almost blushing, looking down at the floor between his legs.'

I-got-the-bullets.

Plato's adoring eyes established the love of the younger boy for his hero. Off-screen, Sal Mineo echoed his Plato, Jim Stark and Jim Dean becoming his role models. He would later describe working with Dean (on *Rebel* and *Giant*) as the most significant experience of his life.

Unhappily, as with others on the *Rebel* set, it was to be a short life. Sal Mineo, by then openly gay, was knifed to death by an unknown killer in Boys Town, LA, at the age of 37. Also to die at 37 was Nick Adams, victim of an overdose after disappointment in both his marriage and career. At 43 years of age Natalie Wood was drowned in a boating accident off Catalina Island, after a career that already fulfilled her early promise. She is remembered above many brilliant performances for her sparkling and tragic Maria in *West Side Story*.

Director Nick Ray was also to be doomed – out of work in his later career after the flawed if fascinating epics, *King of Kings* and *55 Days At Peking*. He became a cult figure, always encouraging to young people [as indeed he encouraged David Sherwin and the author of this book in their first screenplay *Crusaders*, later to become Lindsay Anderson's *If….*]. Nick Ray died after a long and painful battle with lung cancer, a revered if disappointed film-maker.

Rebel Without a Cause was released in October 1955, one month after Dean's death, and the reviews endorsed the high opinions already expressed by those who had worked with him. Even William Zinsser (*New York Herald Tribune*), hating the film, paid tribute to Dean:

> The movie is written and acted so ineptly, directed so sluggishly, that all names but one will be omitted here. The exception is Dean, the gifted young actor who was killed last month. His rare talent and appealing personality even shine through this turgid melodrama.

> The late James Dean reveals completely the talent latent in his *East of Eden* performance. As a new and unwilling member of the gang, a boy who recognised more clearly than any of the others his need for help, he projects the wildness, the torment and the crude tenderness of a restless generation. Gone are the Brando mannerisms, gone too the obvious Kazan touch. He stands as a remarkable talent; and he was cut down, it would seem by the very passions he exposes so tellingly in this strange and forceful picture.
>
> Arthur Knight (the *Saturday Review*)

> Among several fine performances one is unforgettable in its subtlety and strength, the power to suggest by a shrug, an awkward gesture, or hesitant word, an unexpectedly charming smile or suddenly unleashed fury all the loneliness of the young, their dreams and agonised confusions.
>
> Campbell Dixon (*Daily Telegraph*)

Rebel finished shooting in the last week of May 1955. It was the end of a creative partnership which both Nick Ray and James Dean were hoping to continue on future films. There was, as Ray recalls, a strange reluctance on the last evening to pack up and leave the set: 'Jimmy and I were left alone on the lot at Warners; everyone but the gate man had gone home. We were wandering around under the lights making sure we hadn't left anything behind. We didn't really want to admit it was all over. I said, "Let's go. We've nothing more to do here."

'Dean climbed on his motorbike and I climbed in my car and we raced into town very fast. On Hollywood Boulevard he spread himself like a flying angel on the bike with his feet up on the back mudguard, his arms outstretched, and sped off with a roar. Then we stopped at a traffic-light to say goodnight – and even then we couldn't really admit it was all over. So we found an all-night restaurant and had an early breakfast.'

7. Giant

...An actor working on inspiration alone
couldn't do this... He had his own approach
to acting. It was something elusive that
nobody else tried on the screen.

George Stevens

EORGE STEVENS' mammoth production of the Edna Ferber novel, *Giant*, had been in preparation since 1953. When Dean had arrived in Hollywood for *East of Eden* in the spring of 1954, Stevens and his producer Henry Ginsberg were already installed with an office on the Warner's lot, working on the adaptation with script writers, Fred Gill and Ivan Moffat. That this office happened to be situated on Dean's daily path from the dressing room to the *East of Eden* set was pure coincidence. But there had been nothing fortuitous about Dean's habit of dropping in to chat up Stevens' office staff. Dean was well aware of the project under preparation, and ambitious to work with George Stevens, grand master of Hollywood since receiving the Irving Thalberg Memorial Award in 1953, and one of the few directors left who had been making movies since the early 1920s. He had won an Academy Award in 1951 for *A Place in the Sun*, and had won nominations for *The More the Merrier* (1943), and for his most recent, and perhaps most distinguished film, *Shane* (1953).

Dean had learnt the tactics of long drawn-out casting campaigns in his New York days. He had become adept at softening up secretaries, receptionists and assistants, making himself obtrusive or unobtrusive as the occasion demanded. His quiet persistence paid off. By the time work finished on *East of Eden* his name had superceded those of Alan Ladd and Richard Burton on the short list for the part of Jett Rink. Stevens was examining the changes that the casting of Dean would imply in the characterisation, and in the function of the role in the story.

The giants in *Giant* are Texas and the half-million acre Reata ranch, run by brother and sister Bick and Luz Benedict (Rock Hudson and Mercedes McCambridge). The film opens with Bick Benedict arriving in Virginia to stay with a cultured land-owning family, from whom he is buying a horse. He falls in love with the spirited elder daughter of the family, Leslie (Elizabeth Taylor), and ends up with both horse, and the beautiful young Leslie as his bride. He brings her out west to the heat, boredom and bigotry of the Texas cattle lands and the forbidding baroque mansion of the Reata ranch. Jett Rink (James Dean) is one of the Reata hands, disliked for his surly attitudes by Bick Benedict, but favoured by his sister and given the chauffeuring jobs around the ranch. Luz Benedict is the dominant

Jett Rink and the Reata ranch – the image that captured the spirit of Texas.

personality behind the running of the Reata household and she resents the intrusion of her brother's young bride. The resentment is short-lived. Luz is killed out on the prairie, riding the new horse from Virginia. When Bick discovers that she has left a small parcel of land to Jett Rink he tries, without success, to buy the boy out. Jett stays on, and eventually strikes oil on his land. As the Benedict family progress from children (Dennis Hopper, Carroll Baker), to grandchildren, and their corner of Texas from cattle to oil, so Jett Rink becomes the multi-millionaire oil baron, owning towns and airports but obsessed still by his relationship with Bick and Leslie Benedict, and by his love for their daughter, Luz.

As Edna Ferber portrayed him in the book, Jett is a conventional enough version of a tough Texan cow-poke, and Dean seemed the wrong size and image for the part. But Stevens had seen in him the chance to emphasise the element of 'outsider' in Jett Rink: the adopted farm-hand, the runt always excluded from the inner life of the Benedict family. Dean had the particular qualities to express both that state of exclusion and the resulting bitterness that ends up poisoning his whole life.

At first sight Jett Rink seems the odd man out in Dean's three major roles – the conventional rags-to-riches anti-hero of an American fairytale. And yet it completed a pattern: the trilogy of outcast youth, in which *Giant* is the chronological link between the small-town America of *East of Eden* in 1918, and the modern city-dwellers in *Rebel Without a Cause*. Nor was there anything in the vitriolic character of Jett Rink to diminish the James Dean image as rebel hero: even when he finds wealth and power it only serves to expose futility, the empty neon strip at the end of the rainbow. There was none of the diminishment or compromise in this part that was implicit when Marlon Brando dressed up to play his romantic Napoleon in *Desirée*.

Jett Rink could have been Dean's greatest performance. It always promises to be. He starts the film as a peripheral, threatening presence, continually drawing the eye to wherever he lurks, on the edge of the frame, leaning on the verandah, working on the car,

With his patroness Luz Benedict (Mercedes McCambridge).

or dwarfed in the middle-ground of a vast expanse of prairie. His sullen, awkward manner seems to conceal a modicum of good intention and even friendliness. Introduced to Bick's new wife, he mutters and scuffs around in embarrassment, then sticks out a hand in greeting, withdrawing it quickly when she does not respond. Driving her around later in the car, he is her guide into the underside of ranch life, the Mexican shanty town suggesting the kind of childhood he himself has suffered. He reveals vague ambition and restlessness; and each time he is in frame with Elizabeth Taylor, he conveys, as with Julie Harris and Natalie Wood a sensual unease, a threat. The same identification is made: the outsider who is the personification of evil, excitement, disruption or destruction.

In the central section of the film all that suppressed energy is suddenly released. Inheriting his parcel of land Jett paces it out, silhouetted on a skyline, jerky, decisive, savage. When he strikes oil and it comes raining down, blackening him and the surrounding prairie, he leaps into his broken-down old lorry and gatecrashes a Benedict party, driving over their lawns and flowerbeds to throw his triumph and his dirty black challenge in their faces.

But, having established this strong image and presence, Stevens lacked the conviction to allow it to dominate the film. Instead of watching the poison at work, we lose Jett Rink during the formative years of his wealth and power, and whereas the Benedicts can age convincingly enough (despite their silver-blue hair) from children to grandchildren, and from cattle to oil, the sudden transition of Jett, from the solitary cowboy working his own oil drill, to multi-millionaire, leaves the character suspended in mid-air. We no longer know him, and he can no longer convince us that he is real. Dean's portrayal of the ageing alcoholic hardly falters as a piece of acting; it is the dramatisation that lets him down,

Jett Rink introduces Leslie Benedict (Elizabeth Taylor) to the grimmer realities of ranch life.

The trace of oil in the sand (above); black from his 'gusher', Jett gatecrashes a Benedict party (below).

giving him nothing on which to build rapport with the audience. He becomes little more than a cipher in the story.

The dramatic structure in the second half of the film is built round the two themes of frustrated paternal ambition, and racial intolerance: the struggle of Bick Benedict to adapt his old-fashioned prejudice to the fact that his son, Jordan (Dennis Hopper), not only prefers medicine to ranching but has brought home a poor Mexican girl as his bride. The message of racial tolerance is made more palatable in that the girl is, like Jordan, a medical student. A good injun. But Jett Rink enforces his own prejudice, discriminating in his hotels against non-whites, and the final showdown between Jett and Bick at the banquet given in Jett's honour, when his 'heavies' rough up Jordan, help convince Bick that his new-found liberal feelings are worth fighting for. After the epic style and vision of the first half of the film, this contrived melodrama is a sad anti-climax, only kept alive by the vitality of Elizabeth Taylor's performance and the occasional glimpses of Dean and Dennis Hopper. Had the focus of the film remained on Jett, the racial issue at the end could have been more effective, more relevant to his own character, or to his conflict with the Benedicts.

Stevens was altogether more successful with the grandeur of landscape, and only within it do his characters take on life and reality: Bick bringing his new wife home from the rolling green countryside of Virginia; the horrified Leslie, lifting the curtain in their railway sleeping-berth to reveal the car, shunted onto a deserted sideline in the middle of dead and endless prairie and blowing bush-scrub, where, as Bick tells her, 'It's fifty miles to coffee.'

It was essentially as part of this landscape that Stevens used James Dean – a presence as compelling and ominous as the Jack Palance gun-fighter in *Shane*. Consequently Dean's role contained very few sequences of sustained acting, and often the effect of his presence becomes too deliberate. When Luz Benedict dies, Jett's place in the scene is as carefully orchestrated as the groupings of characters in an Antonioni or Renoir film. Technically it was a difficult scene to act, and one that particularly impressed the director of photography, William Mellor: 'In front of camera he [James Dean] had an instinct that was nearly uncanny. I don't recall ever working with anyone who has such a gift... He was in shadow and had to lift his head to the light. We explained how it should go and he played it exactly right to the half-inch first time. He just seemed to know how it should be, without rehearsing or anything.' But once his head is in the light, the focus of attention, the effect becomes too studied: Dean, frozen still in his half-inch lighting margins, and having to overwork his facial muscles to convey the necessary emotion as he surveys the dead body of his patroness.

The two sequences where Dean is given the space and time to develop a scene, work more successfully. Bick and his legal advisers tell Jett about the land Luz has left to him and assume that he will take a cash settlement in exchange. Jett listens to them in silence as they bullshit him, twisting a lariat in his hands, tying a knot in it, looking up and round at them once or twice, near to secret laughter, knowing in himself that he is not going to take their money. Bick Benedict conveys an anger so genuine it is as though Rock Hudson, watching that lariat, knew full well that Dean in his insolent silence was upstaging all of them. Dean walks out at the end of the scene, having refused to part with the land. He is an equal now. A landowner. 'Be seeing ya,' he says, tips his hat at them and splays out his hand palm upwards with a face now openly laughing: 'fuck all of you.'

He creates a quite different mood in a later scene. Leslie Benedict drives past his land and he attracts her attention, firing a gun from up on his water-pump tower. She stops and he invites her into his little shack to entertain her as best he can, nervously making tea, demonstrating reticent pride in his potted plants, sneaking a quick encouraging sip from

Jett refuses to sell out to Bick Benedict (Rock Hudson) the land left to him by Luz.

his hip-flask as she contemplates the fragile dignity of his new independence. The pity is that the elements in the scene are so quickly dissipated in the later contortions of plot. The sexual threat implicit between them is as strong as the sensuality between Cal and Abra in *East of Eden*. Yet the sexual jealousies of Jett and Bick Benedict are never developed beyond their symbolic relevance to what becomes a power struggle between them.

Similarly the boy's social vulnerability gives the audience access to his inner feelings. But compassion for him, and even understanding, are lost as he emerges suddenly the millionaire parvenu. We forget his pain and humiliations. The end of that tea party scene in the shack illustrates the schematisation which finally submerges the characters. As Jett escorts Leslie back to her car, she steps in some soft mud and leaves the imprint that shows him the trace and promise of oil. The development of his character is suddenly reduced to two banalities: the hip-flask in his jeans; and the oil from the sand that will make him rich.

Dean's portrayal of the older Jett Rink has always been the subject of controversy between those who believe that it proved his limitations as an actor and those who claim that it established him as a mature player capable of tackling roles outside his own reality. The performance is all the more difficult to judge because of the deliberate 'ham' mannerisms of the older Jett Rink as he sways carefully through life trying to conceal his chronic drunkenness. Dean had so mastered the physical presence of an older man, that when he met Sal Mineo one day in the studios during costume and make-up tests, Mineo did not recognise him. Dean was so pleased he took Sal Mineo to lunch in the canteen and introduced him to

'The fragile dignity of new independence.' Leslie Benedict visits Jett at Little Reata.

George Stevens. It was as a result of this meeting that Stevens cast Sal Mineo in the part of Angel Obregon II, one of the Mexican boys on the Reata Ranch, whose soldier's funeral after his death in the war is one of the important set pieces at the end of the film.

In the second half of the film Dean was given only one opportunity to express a life and soul in that older millionaire: where, convoluted, self-doubting, self-hating almost, he tries to propose to the Benedicts' daughter, Luz II, in the lush surroundings of his own nightclub. His bowed acceptance of her refusal, and his walk afterwards out into the rain on the terrace, evoke his loneliness and hurt pride, the hopeless empty horizon out in front of him. But how much more telling that would have been if we had known him better as a man. He did not, after all, set out exclusively for wealth and power. They happened to him. Yet the plot manoeuvres us to the nemesis of his downfall.

At the end of the film a banquet is given in his honour. He presides, drunk and incoherent over this last supper, dealing savagely with young Jordan Benedict when the boy confronts him after his Mexican wife has been refused service in the hotel. Two of his heavies hold Jordan while Jett works him over. The enraged Bick Benedict takes Jett out of the banqueting hall, into a huge wine cellar. But the showdown does not materialise. Realising that Jett is incapably drunk, Bick walks out on him and contents himself with ordering his family and friends out of the celebration. Jett Rink returns to the banquet to deliver a speech, but his voice slurs into drunken silence, and he passes out on the table. When he wakes up the banquet is over. He rises to his feet and continues his speech to the darkened empty hall; then finally collapses, crashing over the table, off the dais, into oblivion.

Crucifixion. The most famous publicity still from Giant *– the classic Dean image.*

The film in its failings keeps Jett Rink at arms' length, and if we seem to know him well, it is because our picture is embroidered unavoidably with the parallels in Dean's own life and death. Robert Benayoum, the French critic, wrote:

> Under the exterior of material success he manages to convey a profound moral distress, a fundamental insecurity, which were, moreover, his own. Jett Rink gently rebuffed by the young Luz Benedict brings to mind James Dean's painful rejection by Pier Angeli. What Jett Rink becomes at the height of his triumph is a man assenting to his own destruction. Dead drunk he gives a tortured monologue; and then takes on the immobility of a stone gargoyle. Whether Jimmy Dean would have worn the face he composed here had he lived we shall never know. His old age remains imaginary, mythic, improbable…

Giant was already fifteen days into shooting when Dean joined the unit on 3 June 1955. The introductory scenes had been completed in Charlottesville, Virginia, and the cast was reassembling for the long, hot, exterior sequences to be shot in the prairie, round the small Texan town of Marfa.

The confrontation between Jett Rink and Jordan Benedict (Dennis Hopper) at the banquet given in Jett's honour.

George Stevens rehearses Rock Hudson and James Dean for the final showdown in the wine cellar between Jett and Bick.

Dean had got off to a bad start on the picture so far as discipline and co-operation were concerned. Back in May he had turned up for the pre-production party and press conference in jeans and boots, unshaven, unsmiling and hiding behind shades. He had slumped into a chair and refused to pose for the photographers. The incident became another notorious piece of James Dean folklore, souring his relations with the production before shooting had even begun. But there was a background to Dean's behaviour at this press party, facts that no journalist bothered to explain. The party, a midday lunch, had taken place on 18 May and the production schedule on *Rebel Without a Cause* shows Dean in the middle of a week of night shooting. He arrived at the lunch straight from fifteen hours' work on night exteriors in Griffith Park.

After this shaky start, Stevens was preparing himself for the worst. But during the four weeks' shooting in Texas he had no open disagreements with his temperamental young star.

Accommodation in Marfa was limited, and Dean found himself sharing a house with Rock Hudson, an arrangement perhaps deliberately organised by Stevens to create the undercurrent of hostile familiarity that the men demonstrate in the film, though the conventional Stevens could hardly have anticipated the potential sexual tension between the two actors – Rock Hudson the big, butch, older queen from centre gay frame; James Dean the attractive, androgynous, experimental, experimenting bisexual from the very edge of frame (Rock Hudson was to be one of the first celebrity victims of AIDS in 1985, a death that shocked both the USA and much of Europe into a higher profile attitude towards HIV).

Suffice it to say for *Giant* that the two of them didn't much like one another on or off set. Hudson, like Raymond Massey before him, found Dean's surliness difficult to tolerate, and his 'method' actor's preparations a faintly ludicrous waste of time: 'Before coming on set he used to warm up like a fighter before a contest. He never stepped into camera range without first jumping into the air with his knees up under his chin, or running at full speed around the set shrieking like a bird of prey.'

Like most of the experienced professionals who worked with Dean, Hudson reacted to his unpredictability in rehearsal and performance as though it were some deliberate attempt to upstage and steal scenes. There may well have been an element of mischief or malice in Dean's refusal to play any scene exactly as rehearsed. But it was also essential to his acting technique: there had to be a level of spontaneity in anything that he did, partly to sustain his own adrenalin, partly to avoid the predictable in his reactions, or the reactions of anyone acting with him.

The nightclub scene with young Luz Benedict (Carroll Baker) was rehearsed and shot nearly thirty times during the three days it took to complete. 'There was always something new he would throw in. It was never exactly the same twice over, and I'd have to be listening and watching him just like the girl in the story – a bit tense and apprehensive.'

The unpredictability also upset George Stevens, who could never be quite sure what he was obtaining from any single shot. Dean was by no means infallible, and his continual experimenting gave rise to many mistakes and miscalculations. Stevens always left himself more than well covered in a scene, usually shooting from a minimum of three angles for cutaways or cross-cutting; but there were sequences, and the nightclub scene is one of them, where too much cutting would weaken the scene and where the two-shot or close-up have to be sustained. Stevens would need to scrutinise these takes for any nuance, tone, or gesture that Dean might have changed for the worse; or any detail or dialogue or movement that may have upset continuity. The amount of time Dean needed to prepare himself before each take put further pressure on the director whenever he had doubts about 'printing' or re-shooting.

As the ageing and lonely oil tycoon, Jett Rink re-visits the Benedict house.

An irritability developed between the two of them, building up as the film progressed and hindering their communication at a creative level. Stevens began to react instinctively against Dean's elaborate analysis of scene and character: 'Sometimes he broke a scene down into so many bits and pieces that I couldn't see the scene for the trees, so as to speak. I must admit that I sometimes underestimated him; and sometimes he overestimated the effects he thought he was getting. Then he might change his approach, do it quick, and if that didn't work we'd effect a compromise. All in all it was a hell of a headache to work with him. He was always pulling and hauling, and he had developed this cultivated, designed, irresponsibility. It's tough on you, he'd seem to imply, but I've just got to do it this way. From the director's angle that isn't the most delightful sort of fellow to work with.'

Louis Marcorelles in *Cahiers du Cinema* defined the area of creative disagreement in a later review of the film:

> James Dean curiously enough injects some false notes into the all-too-well-arranged concerto of images and feelings... His style of acting is the very antithesis of the discreet and well-tamed style of the other actors in the film. James Dean unleashes an explosion with his 'caught on the raw' style of acting. It is easy to see why Stevens cordially detested him during filming.

It was this conflict of style that gave the film its dramatic tension, but while Stevens was quite conscious of the effect and fond even of Dean, he could never quite check his impatience enough to build the reciprocal confidence Dean needed in a creative situation.

To Elizabeth Taylor, Stevens seemed at times almost the stern father, feeling himself obliged to punish or restrain: 'He had a kind of love for Jimmy Dean. It was curious to watch him. They'd meet head-on and there'd be a terrible clash. Then when I was not on camera I would watch George watching Jimmy. George would smile, but he didn't ever let Jimmy know that he was fond of him.'

After Dean's death, Stevens was to spend six months, as he said, 'locked up with him', in the cutting-room: 'There was a poetic presence in his every word and gesture. He seemed to be dreaming of some lost tenderness... I can see him now, blinking behind his glasses after having been guilty of some preposterous bit of behaviour and revealing by his very cast of defiance that he felt some sense of unworthiness.'

In retrospect Stevens revised many of his earlier criticisms about Dean. Nine years after he made *Giant*, he described his acting: '... [it was] a mixture of technique, intelligence, and hard work. He gave the impression of being completely natural and improvising as he went along. But no single detail was ever impromptu. He had everything figured out...An actor working on inspiration alone couldn't do this... He had his own approach to acting, it was something elusive that nobody else ever tried on the screen.'

Whether it was influenced by personal animosities, Dean's high opinion of Stevens as a director did not survive the picture. He was used to decisiveness: the enforced economy of filming on a TV set; the conceptual arrogance of Kazan; the instinctual judgements of Nick Ray. Kazan and Ray were both directors who created the shape of their scenes as they filmed, choosing their angles and the punctuation of their shots before they came anywhere near the cutting-room. Detail would inevitably change and the choices would not always work but the visual shape of a scene was predominant in their minds while they were shooting. George Stevens instead would shoot a wide pattern of shots on every scene, accumulating enormous footage to be shaped later during the editing. It was not a system that Dean admired. He derided it to Bill Bast when the unit returned to Hollywood:

> They show up at the beginning of a day's shooting without any real plan. Somehow they sort of muddle through. Stevens has a method I call the 'round the clock' system. He takes all that film and shoots every scene from every possible angle – all round the scene, up, down, here, there – and when he's through he gets himself the best editor in town. Then they spend a year selecting from miles and miles of film the best shots and the best scenes. They figure the whole thing out like a jigsaw puzzle. And when they're through, surprise! – another masterpiece. How can he go wrong?

It was not, needless to say, as effortless and easy as Dean suggested, and Stevens' methods were hardly random or unprepared. Stevens was a little unlucky to catch Dean so sharp;

on the rebound from a director who had given him rare and precocious insight into the techniques of film and the structuring of drama.

After working with Nick Ray, Dean began to express his own ambitions in that direction. It was to become quite normal for a gifted actor to turn towards directing: Brando, Newman, Albert Finney, Richard Attenborough, Jack Lemmon, Jack Nicholson, Robert Redford, Warren Beatty, Clint Eastwood, Sidney Poitier, among many others. But in the Hollywood of the mid-1950s it was unheard of for a young and inexperienced actor to be voicing such ambitions. Agents and producers no doubt smiled indulgently, though there was one young man who not only took Dean's aspirations seriously but believed, and still believes today, that Dean could have fashioned the rebirth of a young American cinema ten years or more before it eventually happened. The young man was Dennis Hopper, whose film *Easy Rider* became the most influential and most successful signal of that eventual renaissance.

James Dean and Dennis Hopper had first met during the making of *Rebel Without a Cause.*

> What we had really was a student-teacher relationship, the only one he ever had, as far as I know. When we were making *Rebel* I just grabbed him one day and said, 'Look man, I gotta know how you act, because you're the greatest!' So he asked me very quietly why I acted, and I told him what a nightmare my home life had been, everybody neurotic because they weren't doing what they wanted to do, and yelling at me when I wanted to be creative, because creative people 'ended up in bars'… Anyway, Jimmy and I found we were both neurotic and had to justify our neuroses by creating, getting the pain out and sharing it. He started watching my takes after that. I wouldn't even know he was there. He'd come up and mumble, 'Why don't you try the scene *this* way.' And he was always right.

This teacher-student relationship continued to even better effect on *Giant*, where Dennis Hopper, in the part of the Benedict son, Jordan Benedict III, had a much larger and more varied role. He would talk to Dean about the psychological realities of the part and the detail of performance and in so doing came nearer than anyone else to understanding the breadth of potential of Dean's creative vision. 'What's wrong with most movie directors is that they understand one aspect of a film, like photography, editing, or acting; but not all the aspects together. Jimmy did. He'd started to refuse to take direction because all he got was bad direction.'

It was ironic that Stevens picked out Dennis Hopper's acting in *Giant* as the 'hottest talent in ten years'.

Apart from Hopper, Dean had few close friends on the set of *Giant*. Down in Marfa he spent most of his free time with his Texan coach, Bob Hinkle, perfecting the roping and riding tricks he had learned with Ted Avery back in 1951. At night the two of them would go off on long hikes across the prairie hunting jack-rabbits and as often as not Dean would be sleeping off the effects of his exertions on set the next day, winning the sympathy of all the actresses in the process. They were not habits that helped cure Stevens of his impatience towards the young star.

But whatever stunts Dean pulled – and for whatever reasons – Liz Taylor remained the undisputed centre of attraction on the unit. She was at twenty-three a queen of Hollywood, the happy wife of Michael Wilding, adored by one and all. And everybody was curious how the young rebel tearaway and the golden star would hit it off together. Bill Bast describes the uneven progress of their relationship:

The day they were introduced, shortly before the picture started, Jimmy was charming, even to the point of taking her for a ride in his new Porsche. His whole approach was contrary to everything she had been braced to expect from him. She went away from that first meeting convinced that people were wrong for referring to him as an anti-social odd-ball. The next time she saw him was on the set [shooting make-up and costume tests]. She approached him in her friendliest manner, expecting from him the same warm reception she had met the first day. Instead she was shocked when Jimmy glared at her over the rims of his glasses, muttered something to himself, and strode off as though he hadn't seen her. She was terribly offended.

As usual when there was an expected pattern to conform to, Dean had broken it, refusing to play the polite admirer. Not that his behaviour made their eventual confrontation in front of camera any easier when work started down in Texas. Dennis Hopper recalls that moment:

Jimmy was doing his first scene with Elizabeth Taylor and it was the first and only time I saw him nervous on set. They were shooting the scene where he fires the shotgun off the water tower, and she stops the car, and he asks her in to tea. He was so uptight he could hardly get the words out. Well there were around four thousand people watching the scene from a hundred yards away, local people and visitors; and all of a sudden Jimmy turned and walked off towards them. He got half-way, unzipped his pants, took out his cock, peed, dripped it off, and zipped it up, and walked back into the scene.

I'd seen him do some weird things, but that was the craziest. And when I asked him why, he said he figured if he could do that in front of four thousand people, he could go back and do anything with Liz Taylor in front of camera.

However disconcerting that incident may have been for her, and however unpredictable his earlier behaviour in Hollywood, Elizabeth Taylor and Dean became close friends during the four weeks on location in Marfa. In common with Julie Harris and Natalie Wood, she has only ever talked about James Dean in terms of affection and regret: 'We were the same age, just a year or so between us: like brother and sister really; kidding all the time, whatever it was we were talking about. One felt he was a boy one had to take care of, but even that was probably his joke. I don't think he needed anybody or anything – except his acting.'

Another friendship that developed on the set, and one that became central to Dean's 'explorative' and intellectual life, was with the stills photographer, Sandford Roth. Sandy and

Beulah Roth had only recently returned from Europe, and Dean would listen for hours as they talked about the writers and artists they had met there and about Europe as a place to live and work. The two of them took the place of Dean's New York friends as his teachers and counsellors, and with them he would talk of his ambitions and plans.

Relations between Stevens and Dean moved onto collision course when the unit returned to Hollywood in early July. In Marfa there had been few distractions off-set and, apart from Dean's nocturnal hunting trips, no problems of punctuality or discipline. Compared to the interior scenes that were to follow, Dean's share of work in the location sequences had been very high, and there were only a few days when he had not appeared on camera. Back in the studios, there were all too many occasions when Dean, made-up and 'psyched-up' for a scene, would spend all day kicking his heels and doing nothing. On *East of Eden* and *Rebel* his presence on screen had been around nine-tenths of the total running time, while on *Giant* the ratio was down to only one-tenth. The frustration and boredom began to annoy him and he developed a system with one of the production staff whereby he was told, quite unofficially, whether or not he would be required for the day's work. Stevens found out about this system and reprimanded him. Dean in his turn demanded to be given a proper timetable of work-days and off-days and for a few weeks peace was restored. But inevitably the schedule came under pressure and last minute alterations had to be made. Dean found himself, once again hanging around with nothing to do. He told Hedda Hopper: 'I sat there for three days, made up and ready to work at nine o'clock every morning. By six o'clock I hadn't had a scene or a rehearsal. I sat there like a bump on a log watching that big lumpy Rock Hudson making love to Liz Taylor. I'm not going to take it any more.'

He reverted to his private system with another spy in the production office, turning up at the studios only when he was sure he would be required on set. But this time his system came unstuck. Mercedes McCambridge had a fall one morning and cut her face. The schedule had to be switched; Dean was nowhere to be found. Stevens spent the rest of the morning on rehearsals, and in the lunch-break Elizabeth Taylor drove off in her car to find the truant actor. She knew Dean was in the process of moving into a new house in the San Fernando valley and, having located him there, she brought him back in time for the afternoon's work. When Dean walked on set after lunch Stevens let fly at him in front of the whole unit, telling him there was no place in Hollywood for his type and that it would be a welcome relief for everyone if he packed his bags and returned to New York.

Dean seemed to shrug off the incident, and worked out the day co-operatively enough. But later the same week, in a moment of anger or disillusion, he contemplated taking Stevens' words at face value. No one is clear how close Dean came to walking off the picture, but he certainly had a long talk about it with Hedda Hopper. She recalled their conversation in her autobiography *The Whole Truth and Nothing But*:

> [I told him] I hold no brief for Stevens, but what you don't know is that there's a man on that set who put the whole deal together. Henry Ginsberg, Stevens, and Edna Ferber are partners. It took Henry two years to do it. This is the first time in Ferber's life she took no money, only an equal share of the profits as they come in. If this picture goes wrong Stevens can walk out and those two years of Ginsberg's life go down the drain…. Something else. Henry has a great deal of affection for you, but he can't show it or else Stevens might walk off the set.

Dean returned to work without further demonstration and kept quietly to his call sheet and schedule during the remaining weeks of work, though it was noticeable that on the days he was called on set Stevens never again kept him waiting.

James Dean with Ursula Andress at a party.

But his behaviour had antagonised many of the technicians on the unit. When Dean apologised about the absence that had caused the morning's delay, there was no hint of acceptance from any of them. Dean waited in the silence and finally said: 'Maybe I better go to the moon.'

'We'll help you pack,' one of them replied; and for the remaining month or so of work he was ostracised by them all. They sometimes applauded his acting, but they never spoke to him off-set. Their reaction puzzled and hurt him more than he cared to admit.

It was just as well that friendship with the Roths had given a new focus to his Hollywood life. During the 'Jekyll and Hyde' period before *Rebel,* and during this unsettled time working on *Giant,* Dean found himself losing friends. Even Len Rosenman had quarrelled with him. The two of them were old friends from New York, and it was through Dean that Rosenman had met Kazan and been commissioned for the music on *East of Eden.* He was now working on the music track for *Rebel* – a score so difficult that a Hollywood trade paper reported, 'The Warners Studio Orchestra is doing it in three sessions, three weeks apart. Intervals are for rehearsals.' Although Rosenman was only a few years older than him, Dean had adopted him first as teacher and counsellor, then as father, elder brother, or younger brother, as the mood took him. But the unpredictability of these moods was a great strain for any friendship and Dean's spasmodic bouts of violence, usually the result of drinking too much, finally caused Rosenman to break with him.

It was this same unpredictability of mood and behaviour that had helped undermine his love affair with Pier Angeli and which now threatened his short-lived relationship with Ursula Andress. The Swiss-born actress was a glamorous newcomer to the Hollywood scene in that summer of 1955 and she met up with Dean sometime after his return from

Texas: 'He came by my house late. He came in room like wild animal, and smell of everything I don't like. We go hear jazz music and he leave table. Say he go play drums. He no come back. I don't like to be alone. I go home. He come by my home later and say he sorry. Ask if I want to see his motorsickle. We sit on sidewalk in front of motorsickle and talk, talk, talk, until five.'

Like Pier Angeli, Ursula Andress had come to Hollywood from Rome, though unlike Pier she had been involved there with the Bohemian *ambiente* of existentialist writers and artists. She was outspoken and unconventional, characteristics which appealed to Dean; but she was also argumentative beyond anything he had experienced before in a girl. Alone of all his girlfriends she would not accept the eccentricities of his behaviour, unless he could convince her that there was a good reason behind it, and at any level of conversation, in private or public, they would argue and debate incessantly.

> Jimmy Dean is studying German so that he can fight with Ursula Andress in two languages. Jimmy says he likes Ursula because she talks back.
>
> The *Hollywood Reporter,* 12 August 1955

But whatever the tittle-tattle of gossip, the reality of their relationship was conducted away from the parties or night-clubs where the columnists operated. They rarely attended public functions together, and according to his friends the two of them spent most of their free time on their own. No one, except Ursula Andress herself, can really know how serious their love affair was, nor how emotionally involved Dean had become by the time she left him for John Derrick.

If one can believe the columnists and the claims of reminiscences, he was also at this time dating Lili Kardell and her room-mate, Claire Kelly, and he had certainly for some time been friendly with Maila Nurmi, the actress who played Vampira in the TV series of the same name. Their friendship had started with Dean's curiosity about the occult and the claims made by Vampira, or by the *Vampira* publicity machine, that she had genuine gifts of 'spiritual communication'. Dean was disappointed in both her knowledge and her gifts in that particular direction; but he came to value instead her warmth and compassion as a friend. He probably confided more of his true feelings through these troubled months with her, than with any of his other close friends.

She endorses a general impression of Dean during that September: 'Towards the end of *Giant* he really cut off all private relationships, except for Ursula Andress, while that lasted. He was withdrawn and largely self-sufficient, his new home in the San Fernando Valley known around Hollywood as his sanctuary of isolation.' His free time was taken up with clay-modelling under the tutelage of the sculptress Pegot Waring; with the contemplation of sports cars and motorcycles; and with books and records in his untidy studio. Nicholas Ray likened his mood at this time to the aloof neurosis of a Siamese cat: 'There are times when it withdraws completely, the world seems too much to bear and it becomes restless, morose and unassailable; there are times when it appeals, with an almost helpless docility, for sympathy and attention. Its actions suggest a creature that has never become truly domesticated, that carries atavistic memories or intuitions of a freer, less perplexing life. It is not really at ease with the world in which it has to live, sometimes it tries to reject it altogether – but it always comes back, because there is no other.'

Ray's allusion to the Siamese cat referred to the pet that shared Dean's San Fernando retreat during the last weeks of his life. Sometime in August or September, perhaps to compensate in some way for the trouble between Dean and the unit on *Giant*, Liz Taylor had made him a present of a Siamese kitten, and Ray, as so often, was the expert to whom Dean turned for advice. 'The last time I saw James Dean was when he arrived without warning at

The last supper. Jett Rink presides drunk and incoherent, finally collapsing over the table into oblivion.

my Hollywood home about three o'clock in the morning. That evening we had met for dinner. We had talked for several hours of many things, of future plans, including a story called *Heroic Love* that we were going to do. When he reappeared later he had been given a Siamese cat by Elizabeth Taylor, and he wanted to borrow a book of mine on cats before driving home.'

Dean found out from Ray's book that the Siamese cat needs happiness as well as a correct diet. It is, he read, potentially a very neurotic animal. He took to staying in nights to keep 'young Marcus' company. He would even drive home in the lunch-break to feed it. But he eventually decided he could not cope with its emotional needs. 'I might go out some night and never come home,' he told the Roths. 'Then what would happen to Marcus?' Dean gave him away to one of his girlfriends. Inevitably, the story was told around Hollywood that on the night of Dean's death the kitten disappeared and was never seen again.

Dean finished his 'last supper' scene in *Giant* on 22 September. On the evening of the 27th, he was called back to the studios to look at the rushes. George Stevens introduced the sequence to the audience in the viewing theatre, members of the cast, studio executives and a few guests. He described it as one of the most difficult scenes ever undertaken by a screen actor.

Dean arrived characteristically late for the showing, walking in just as the lights came up at the end. He told Nick Adams next day, 'they were all wet-eyed so it must have been good' (technically it was far from perfect: Dean mumbled so badly in his takes that the scene had to be re-dubbed after his death with Nick Adams impersonating Dean's voice).

Dean said goodbye that evening to George Stevens outside the viewing theatre: 'Now it's all over, we don't have to bug each other no more. And I can go back to my motor racing.' No hard feelings, he was maybe trying to say.

Those 'last supper' takes were shown on a Tuesday. It was in the middle of Friday night's rushes that they rang George Stevens in the same viewing theatre to tell him James Dean had been killed.

Giant was released in October 1956, more than a year after Dean's death. It won an Oscar for George Stevens, nominations for James Dean and Rock Hudson, and became, notwithstanding its five and a half million dollar budget, one of Warner Brothers' biggest financial successes. The matinee audiences queued to see Rock Hudson and Elizabeth Taylor in a grand old-fashioned romance; while the younger audience queued, with less respect for the film or the story, to see James Dean. And by and large the critics praised him, at a time when many of them might have welcomed the chance to deflate his reputation, not out of malice, but to bring perspective to a legend already inflated and macabre.

Courtland Phipps in *Films in Review* had obviously had enough both of the legend, and the acting style:

> … [Elizabeth Taylor's] scenes with an off-hand ranch-hand… were rendered pointless by James Dean's one and only successful acting style – the loutish and malicious petulance which present-day teenagers profess to admire. Dean made the young Jett Rink such a boor not even a wife more neurotic than the one Miss Taylor was portraying could have thought him attractive.
>
> Since Dean is dead I shall say nothing about his attempts to portray the mature Jett Rink, except to say it is embarrassing to see.

Bosley Crowther of the *New York Times*, hitherto an anti-Dean critic, had been expected to write a similarly harsh comment. Instead Dean's performance changed his opinion:

It is the late James Dean who makes this malignant role the most tangy and corrosive in the film. Mr Dean plays this curious villain with a stylised spookiness – a sly sort of off-beat languor and slur of language – that concentrates spite. This is a haunting cap-stone to the brief career of Mr Dean.

The usually cautious *Time* magazine, while deeply critical of the posthumous and hysterical Dean legend in an earlier article, spoke of 'genius' in its appraisal of *Giant*:

James Dean who was killed in a sports car crash two weeks after his last scene in *Giant* was shot, in this film clearly shows for the first (and fatefully the last) time what his admirers always said he had: a streak of genius. He has caught the Texas accent to nasal perfection and mastered that lock-hipped, high-heeled, stagger of the wrangler, and the wry little jerks and smirks, tics and twitches, grunts and giggles that make up most of the language of a man who talks to himself a good deal more than he does to anyone else. In one scene, indeed, in a long drunken mumble with actress Carroll Baker... Dean is able to press an amazing array of subtleties into the mood of the movement, to achieve what is certainly the finest piece of atmospheric acting seen on the screen since Marlon Brando and Rod Steiger did their 'brother' scene in *On the Waterfront*.

Parallels between the actor and his screen personality were never far below the surface. Jean Queval, writing in *Télécine*, described Dean's signature to the character of Jett Rink – a characteristic that could have been James Dean's own personal salutation.

There is one gesture which is unforgettable – a gesture which recurs as the *leit-motive*. The right hand held out open, palm up, and insolently swung to the side – the gesture that says: 'count me out'; that indicates withdrawal. And the gesture is emphasised by blue eyes which mock rather than challenge; the gesture of one who is retreating deep into himself, misunderstood, arrogant, and invulnerable.

8. Death in the Afternoon

> The only place where you could see life and
> death, i.e. violent death now that the wars
> were over, was in the bullring…
>
> *Hemingway*

HEMINGWAY'S words in the first chapter of his textbook on bullfighting, *Death in the Afternoon*. James Dean had underlined the sentence with a red pen in his copy of the book.

In chapter four Hemingway describes the death of a young bullfighter, Manuel Granero:

> He was twenty years old when he was killed by a Veragua bull that lifted him once, then tossed him against the wood of the foot of the barrera and never left him until the horn had broken up the skull as you might break a flower-pot. He was a fine-looking boy who studied the violin until he was fourteen, studied bullfighting until he was seventeen and fought bulls until he was twenty.

There is a photograph of Granero in the book, on the horns, and dying. Opposite the photograph Dean had inscribed four words, each of them underlined in a different colour: 'disability' in green; 'disfigurement' in blue; 'degradation' in yellow; 'death' in red. Selected passages throughout the rest of the book were marked in one or other of the four colours. Inside the book was a cutting from a Mexican magazine describing the death of Manolete in the bullring and a typewritten sheet of paper with two verses from Lorca's lament for another dead bullfighter, Ignacio Sánchez Mejias:

> At five in the afternoon.
> It was exactly five in the afternoon.
> A boy brought the white sheet
> *at five in the afternoon*
> A basket of lime ready prepared
> *at five in the afternoon*
> The rest was death and death only
> *at five in the afternoon.*

'V' for victory – clowning around in the coffins in Vernor Hunt's General Store, Fairmount .

As a nine-year-old boy Dean had watched his mother die. He was intimate with death; it was a reality to him of physical decay and deep personal loss, and, whatever theories on the nature of mortality the Rev De Weerd may have impressed upon him, Dean remained obsessed by it: hypnotised; afraid; touching it and analysing it as though it could be defined; clowning in open coffins to exorcise it with laughter; idealising it to take away the fear or the mystery.

He was once asked in an interview: 'What is the thing you respect above all else?'

'That's easy. Death. It's the only thing left to respect. It's the one inevitable, undeniable truth. Everything else can be questioned. But death is truth. In it lies the only nobility for man, and beyond it the only hope.'

When the photo-journalist, Robert Capa, was killed by a landmine in Vietnam, Dean obtained a cutting of Capa's most famous picture, the Spanish loyalist in the Civil War, his arms and rifle outflung, caught by the camera in the very moment a bullet kills him. Dean inscribed the picture with the date and place of Capa's own death: 'Doai Than, afternoon, May 25th 1954.' He sat up throughout the night before the Rosenbergs were electrocuted in Sing Sing, reading Oscar Wilde's *Ballad of Reading Jail* (he would later remark of his 'make-up' in *Giant*, that they had fashioned him, as the ageing Jett Rink, in the image of Julius Rosenberg).

Granero, Manolete, Mejias, Capa, the Rosenbergs, the Italian racing driver Alberto Ascari: he collected the deaths that were significant to him in much the same way that others came subsequently to possess his death. With such a macabre obsession it was hardly strange that Dean had premonitions of his own early death. Many others have, in some fit of paranoia or excess of narcissism, convinced themselves that 'those whom the Gods love die young', the foreboding suggested between Jim Stark and Judy in *Rebel Without a Cause*:

JIM: You know something? I never figured I'd live to see eighteen. Isn't that dumb?

JUDY: No.

JIM: Each day I'd look in the mirror and I'd say, 'What, you still here?'

For Dean it was not so much a 'death wish', as an overpowering consciousness of the proximity and inevitability of death.

A photographer, Frank Worth, visited Dean at his San Fernando home during that last week of September 1955, and heard some tapes Dean was playing around with: 'They gave me the creeps. They were all about death and dying, poems and things he just made up. They were his ideas on what it might be like to die, and how it would feel to be in the grave and all that.'

A National Highways Committee road safety commercial was shot with Dean on a neighbouring sound stage during his final day of retakes on *Giant*. In it he is dressed as the young Jett Rink, complete with the hat and the lariat, chatting to the interviewer (actor, Gig Young) about cars, about his success on the race track and about the dangers of fast driving on the highway. His parting words on the film, delivered into camera and pointing at himself, proved in retrospect a grim irony:

'Remember take it easy driving – the life you might save might be *mine*.'

He signed off the clip at the doorway with that odd gesture of farewell he had invented for Jett Rink – the upturned palm swung to and fro as though he was trying to show the audience something invisible to anyone but himself.

That last week in September 1955 Dean's future seemed full of promise and excitement.

As Jim Stark in Rebel, *'You know something? I never figured I'd live to see eighteen.'*

NBC had signed him up in a TV epic (with an unprecedented fee for television of $20,000) to be filmed that October. Warner Brothers were lining up his next film, agreeing to release him to MGM, in return for the loan of Liz Taylor on *Giant*. At MGM Dean was to play the New York boxer, Rocky Graziano, in the film based on his life story, *Somebody Up There Likes Me* (Paul Newman inherited the part after Dean's death, co-starring, ironically with Pier Angeli; Newman also took over the Billy the Kid role in *The Left-Handed Gun* that had been set aside for Dean). Jane Deacy had arrived in Hollywood towards the end of the month to negotiate a $900,000 contract with Warners (nine films in six years), which included provision for a twelve-month sabbatical to start sometime during 1956.

Dean had his own conflicting ambitions for those free twelve months. He told Jane Deacy and Hedda Hopper that he wanted to play Hamlet: 'Only a young man can play him as he was – with the naivety. Laurence Olivier plays it safe. Something is lost when the older men play him. They anticipate the answers. You don't feel that Hamlet is thinking – just declaiming. Sonority of voice and technique the older men have, but this kind of Hamlet isn't the stumbling, feeling, reaching, searching boy he really was.'

He told Pegot Waring he would spend the year carving giant sculptures in the Grand Canyon. He told Sandy and Beulah Roth he would take a long vacation and tour Europe. And he told Rolf Weutherich he was planning twelve months total dedication to motor racing, for which he'd ordered a Lotus Mark IX sports car from England – no road production model this time, but a fully fledged track car.

After his various frustrations on *Giant*, and after his enforced four-month suspension from all racing activities, it was scarcely surprising if his immediate ambitions were turned in that direction. There was a race meeting in Salinas coming up at the end of the month, and when Dean was shown a $6,000 competition Porsche in the agent's showroom, he walked in and bought it without a second thought. The '550 Spyders' were rare specimens, and he knew he would be waiting months for his Lotus to be shipped out from England.

He ran the new car around Hollywood during the few days left before the Salinas race meeting, with every intention of running-in the engine before it was subjected to the stresses of racing speeds. But his week turned out to be congested. The car had to be checked over by his mechanic Rolf Weutherich; Jane Deacy was in town; his uncle and aunt had come out from Indiana to stay for a few days with Winton Dean in Santa Monica. By the time Thursday came there were only a hundred or so miles on the clock, and Dean told Weutherich that if the weather was fine next day they may as well drive the Porsche to Salinas, instead of loading it on the trailer (apart from the tuned engine and the lightweight body the Porsche was a standard road-equipped car).

He was in a festive mood. This resumption of racing was an occasion to celebrate and he wanted his friends to come along with him. He called them all, without much success, on Thursday and Friday morning: Bill Bast; Nick Ray; the Roths; Nick Adams; Dick Davalos; Len Rosenman and Rosenman's nephew, Lew Bracker, the insurance salesman and motor racing fanatic who had become a close friend of Dean over those last few months.

Lew Bracker was negotiating an insurance policy on Dean's behalf, and he visited him at his San Fernando home on the Thursday or Friday, asking Dean to nominate the beneficiaries for the policy. Dean told him to set down his grandparents in Fairmount for $5,000 each; his nephew Marcus for $10,000; and the remainder of the $100,000 policy for his uncle and aunt, Marcus and Ortense. Bracker advised him instead to draw up a proper will, and make his estate the beneficiary for the insurance policy. Dean accordingly arranged an appointment with a lawyer for the following week (in the absence of a will at the time of the accident his assets all passed to the next of kin, his father, the one close relative who was not, for whatever reason, accidental or otherwise, nominated in that list of beneficiaries).

Jane Deacy, and Dean's uncle and aunt had left town; Bill Bast was busy on a new TV

Jimmy in his new Porsche, a few days before his death.

play that Dean was helping to finance; Rosenman was working; Nick Ray was in London; and Nick Adams and Dick Davalos were in New York. Besides the mechanic the only two friends coming north to Salinas with him were Sandy Roth and another motor racing fanatic, Bill Hickman. Dean gave them the Ford station-wagon with the trailer to tow, while he and Weutherich took the Porsche. The silver sports car already had Dean's racing number taped or painted in black on the side, 130, together with the nickname Dean had given the car, 'The Little Bastard'.

On Friday 30 September they set out around two in the afternoon taking the Ridge Route (then numbered Highway 99) north out of Los Angeles, stopping for a snack at a roadside diner. Coming through Bakersfield both cars were flagged down by a traffic cop and given speeding tickets for clocking sixty-five in a forty-five zone. 'Take it easy,' the cop told Dean, 'else you won't even make Salinas.' Dean told him: 'I can't get her to run right at under eighty.' He called back to Sandy Roth in the station-wagon: 'See you for dinner in Paso Robles.'

At around five o'clock Dean spotted a Mercedes 300 SL parked at Blackwell's Corner. He pulled in for a look at the car, and talked for a few moments with its owner Lance Reventlow, son of Barbara Hutton. Reventlow was also on his way north for the race meeting in Salinas. Dean showed him the speeding ticket.

'And I just done a road safety film. Some fucking journalist is going to love to pick that up.'

It was some time between 5.40 and 5.50 at the junction of Highway 466 and 41 on an empty flat road, with the light beginning to fade. A black Plymouth limousine driven by a twenty-three-year-old student, Donald Turnupseed and travelling south-east on 466, pulled across the road to turn north-east onto 41. 'He's gotta stop,' shouted Dean. 'He's gotta see us.'

But it would seem that the other driver, if he saw the low and unlit silver car at all, saw it too late. He was in the middle of his turn and blocking Dean's road when the lightweight sports car smashed into the Plymouth and crumpled up like paper. Rolf Weutherich was badly injured but thrown clear. Dean was trapped in the cockpit, pinned behind the wheel.

The trailer-car with Sandy Roth and Bill Hickman arrived five, maybe ten minutes later. An ambulance had already been called. Donald Turnupseed was wandering around in a state of shock, but virtually unharmed. He kept repeating to everyone: 'I didn't see him.' Rolf Weutherich was lying unconscious on the verge with a badly fractured skull and a broken leg. Sandy Roth took pictures of the two cars in case they were needed for evidence: the pictures he has never shown to anyone are those taken of Dean trapped unconscious in the crumpled Porsche during the interminable wait for the ambulance. His head and face were apparently unmarked; but his neck was broken, and his body torn open on the steering-wheel, like a bullfighter on the horns.

According to medical evidence James Dean died in the ambulance on the way to hospital without regaining consciousness.

A few minutes after the ambulance left the scene two police patrol cars arrived to start compiling an accident report: Captain Tripke and Officer Nelson. They had received their message over the police radio at 5.59, notification probably coming from the ambulance station at Cholame, a mile or so east of the intersection where the accident occurred. It was estimated that around five minutes elapsed between the moment of the accident and the call for an ambulance, the time it took for some passing motorist to reach the nearest telephone. Another five to seven minutes passed before Dean was extracted from the wreck. Captain Tripke arrived at the intersection some twenty minutes after the accident had happened. He found an anxious crowd of people, some of whom had already identified the wrecked Porsche. Most of them were also motor racing fans or competitors on their way to the meeting at Salinas. In a later interview Captain Tripke remembered the confusion: 'I had never heard of James Dean, the movie star. After much thought and pondering in my mind I felt it was Jimmy Dean who sang cowboy and western songs... I kept getting radio calls asking about him. And when I got to the hospital later in the evening every phone in the place was ringing, and all the lights were flashing and we had news media calling from all over.'

The two policemen had found the Plymouth still parked at the point of impact in the junction. The Porsche was further up the road, on the north shoulder of 466. There were thirty to forty feet of skid marks on the Porsche path to impact.

Every fact relating to the accident became a source of subsequent controversy. Different theories were claimed by journalists: that Dean was driving recklessly fast; that he was not wearing his spectacles; that the accident resulted from his aggressive reluctance to give way to another car; that he was not the driver at all, but that Weutherich was behind the wheel when they crashed.

Inevitably the established facts take us only half-way. They are in themselves only theories: the official theories. A coroner's inquest was held the following week in Paso Robles (and adjourned to the city auditorium because of the large amount of spectators who could not be accommodated in the normal court). An open verdict was returned: contributory negligence on both sides.

The police evidence mentioned the possibility of low sun in Dean's eyes and the silver colour and low profile of the Porsche. Calculations had also been made by Captain Tripke concerning Dean's estimated speed: 'In order to present all the facts at the inquest we felt it only fair to backtrack on him as well as on the other driver... We found Dean had received a speeding citation over on Highway 99, coming off the Grapevine. And in checking the time on the citation and the mileage covered to the accident scene... we found that if he'd taken the most direct route and not stopped at all we would have had to average 69 mph...Further investigation revealed that he did not take the most direct route but took Highway 99 up through Bakersfield, right through town and the commuter hour traffic, then continued north on 99 to Vermosa, before coming west on 46. He stopped at Blackwell's Corner, ate an apple and drank a Coke, and entered into conversation with various people around there. He tried to get a fellow in a Corvette to race with him – the fellow in the Corvette did not wish to. With all these deviations and the stop he still averaged 69 mph.'

There is no doubt that Dean had been driving very fast. The Porsche had a maximum speed, depending on its gearing, of between 100 and 110, and Weutherich would probably have advised a maximum running-in speed of 70 to 80.

Beyond the factor of speed the accident was caused either by Turnupseed not picking up the fast moving low profile and neutral coloured Porsche, or by a simple misunderstanding of intention. A later account (probably based on a reconstruction of events by Weutherich) suggested that Turnupseed stopped in the middle of the junction before making the turn, and that he carried on with the manoeuvre ('lurching forward' was the phrase used) because he thought that the Porsche was slowing down for him. A 'lurching forward' could also have been caused if the driver's foot had slipped off the clutch pedal. Dean's late braking marks would also support the theory of some last-second change in the position of the other car.

Any of the more melodramatic theories can be excluded. Whatever Dean's premonitions of death, and whatever the talk afterwards of suicide, voluntary or involuntary, there was no ambiguity about the manner of his death. He was full of ambitious plans, and, in contrast to his usual post-film depression, possessed of *joie de vivre*. He was one of the 38,300 Americans who died that year on the roads, unnecessarily, quite arbitrarily.

James Dean's body was officially identified by his father, Winton Dean, at a morgue in Paso Robles later the same night.

The news filtered through Hollywood during the evening. The cast on *Giant* were in the viewing theatre, and Elizabeth Taylor later recalled the scene in her autobiography, *An Informal Memoir*:

> Suddenly the phone rang. I heard him [George Stevens] say, 'No, my God. When? Are you sure?' And he kind of grunted a couple of times and hung up the phone. He stopped the film and turned on the lights, stood up and said to the room, 'I've just been given the news that Jimmy Dean has been killed.'

> There was an intake of breath. No one said anything. I couldn't believe it; none of us could. So several of us started calling newspapers, hospitals, police, the morgue. The news was not general at that time. After maybe two hours the word was confirmed.

> Then everybody drifted out to their cars to go home. It was about nine o'clock at night; the studio was deserted. As I walked to my car, feeling numb, I saw a figure coming through the lights down one of the little side-streets. It was George, getting into his Mercedes. We looked at each other, and I said, 'I can't believe it, George. I can't believe it.' He said, 'I believe it. He had it coming to him. The way he drove, he had it coming.'

Elizabeth Taylor later collapsed, from shock or nervous strain, and was taken to hospital.

Natalie Wood was in New York, where she had been working on promotion for *Rebel Without a Cause*, and rehearsing a TV show:

> The night he was killed I was having dinner with a lot of his friends – Sal Mineo, Nick Adams, Dick Davalos. We were talking about Jimmy's lifestyle and Nick ventured the opinion that Jimmy wouldn't live to thirty. We pooh-poohed the idea. But he said Jimmy was attracted to a lot of dangerous sports: motor racing, motor bikes, bullfighting, rodeos.
>
> Later, when we finished eating, Nick and Sal walked me to my hotel. I was still under age then, with a studio chaperon; and it was she who heard the news. She told Nick and Sal and asked them not to say anything to me because I had an early call next day and she wanted me to sleep. So they left rather abruptly.

> Next morning the chaperon had to tell me, because down in the lobby all the newspapers had it on headlines. I didn't believe it. I think I stood at the window staring out for a long time. I went to work in a state of shock. [Natalie Wood was due to perform that day on a live two-and-a-half-hour television show, *Heidi*]. I was sharing a dressing room with Jo Van Fleet – she had been Cal's mother in *East of Eden*. She hadn't heard about it, and when they told her she collapsed on the stairs. We were both in such a state everyone thought they'd have to cancel the show. Jo was the strong one. She said we must pull ourselves together and not think about it until afterwards. It was because of her I didn't go to pieces.

The wreckage of Dean's Porsche on Highway 466.

Dean's body was flown to Indiana on the Tuesday after the accident. He was buried back home in Fairmount on the following Saturday, 8 October. The funeral service was held in the Friends' Back Creek Church, the congregation inside and outside the church far outnumbering the population of the small town.

Henry Ginsberg (producer on *Giant*), Steve Brooks (Warner Brothers), and Stewart Stern (script-writer on *Rebel*), were, it seems, the only three representatives from Hollywood.

The service was taken by the Pastor Xen Harvey, and by Dean's old friend the methodist minister, Rev James De Weerd, who flew in specially from a previous commitment in Cincinnati and was escorted to the church by a State Police patrol car. Xen Harvey concluded the eulogy with these words:

The career of James Dean has not ended. It has just begun. And God Himself is directing the production.

But no God could have planned the macabre aftermath to Dean's death. Nor would Dean himself have wished for such a grotesque mortality.

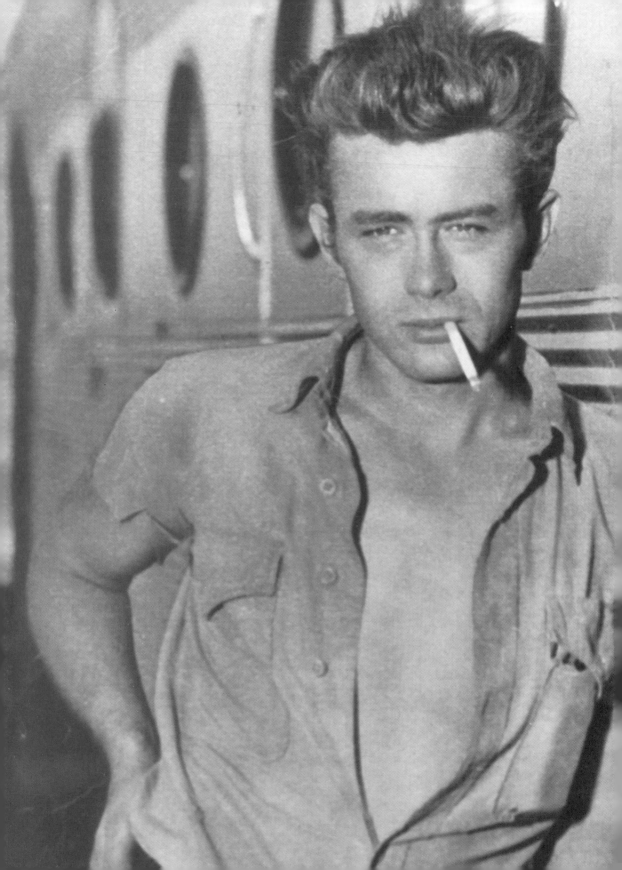

9. Debris and a Legend

America has known many rebellions –
but never one like this: millions of
teenage rebels heading for nowhere,
some in 'hot-rod' cars, others on the
blare of rock 'n'roll music, some with
guns in their hands. And at their
head – a dead leader.

Picture Post, 8 October 1956

EAST OF EDEN had already established James Dean as the governing image of a restless, rootless generation and neither his violent death nor the release of his subsequent films would do anything to diminish his stature as rebel king. Edgar Morin wrote in *Presence du Cinema*:

One part of the youth of the world recognised itself as though in a mirror in the face of that young hero. By his death James Dean became the full hero: death had authenticated his *fureur de vivre,* and the adolescent's challenge to life, that is always a challenge to death.

James Dean was now untouchable and death enclosed the image in a grisly necrolatry.

Initial reaction in Hollywood was guarded. The precedents were bad. The deaths of Carole Lombard, Jean Harlow, Leslie Howard and John Garfield had killed their films at the box office, and Warner Brothers was certain that the same fate awaited Dean's two unreleased pictures. Natalie Wood had already been working on the pre-release publicity for *Rebel Without a Cause* (due for an October opening), giving TV and newspaper interviews in New York and Hollywood. She experienced the studio reaction first hand: 'Warner Brothers' immediate reaction was that it could only be a catastrophe and they tried to cancel the premiere. Jack Warner said they were finished with these two films – "nobody will come and see a corpse", he said. Then there was this counter-reaction. To their amazement *Rebel* came out and was a huge success despite what had happened.'

The columnist, Hedda Hopper, was one of the first figures in the Hollywood establishment to realise the nature and extent of public reaction to Dean's death: 'Only once before had anything equalled the mail that deluged my office, and that came after Rudolph Valentino died. Letters mourning Jimmy came by the thousands week after week. They came from young and old alike, some crisply typewritten, some pencil scrawls, and they kept coming three years after. He was an extraordinary boy and people sensed the magnetism. He stood on the threshold of manhood, the adolescent yearning to grow, trying to find himself, and millions know that feeling.'

Warners were similarly inundated with fan mail, some of it so morbid that the Studio eventually called in psychiatrists to analyse the letters.

Jimmy darling, I know you are not dead. I know you are just hiding, because your face has been disfigured in the crash. Don't hide Jimmy. Come back. It won't matter to us.

When James Dean was killed in that horrible accident it seemed like a big black curtain had been drawn in my life. But he will never die, no, not the great James Dean. He can't.

I was wondering if you would send me a piece of his clothing. Just a piece, so I will have something. Even if it's just a piece of his hair when he was small. I don't care what you send just as long as it is something.

… Some day I'll even meet Jim if the Lord wants me to. And I'm sure he won't object. There is only one thing I can't believe – that Jim is dead. I don't know why, but I just can't.

For three years following his death, letters addressed to Dean continued to outnumber the fan mail of any living Hollywood star, despite the fact that Warners did little outside the normal publicity for *Rebel* and *Giant* to encourage the legend. They refused to sponsor or even recognise an official fan club, and their only concession to the Dean public was a special office and secretarial pool to answer the mail and send out photographs.

But the fringe opportunists of showbiz recognised a gilt-edged legend. Where Warners refused to exploit there were a dozen publishers or record companies ready to cash in. Bootleg records were issued of Dean's tapes, and pop records were brought out with his photograph on the cover and songs dedicated to or written about him: *A Boy Named James Dean; Hymn for James Dean; James Dean is Not Dead; The Ballad of James Dean; Jimmy, Jimmy; The Racer Lives Forever; The Story of James Dean; His Name Was Dean; Goodbye My Jamie Boy; Goodbye to You James Dean; Jimmy Dean's Christmas in Heaven.*

Magazines ran sensational or gossip articles on the dead actor: *Is Natalie Wood Betraying Jimmy Dean?; Jimmy Dean Suicide Rumours; Did Jimmy Dean Leave a Son?; Did Jimmy Dean Really Die?; Jimmy Dean's Hidden Heartbreak; Death Drive; I Almost Married Jimmy Dean; The Ghost Who Wrecked Pier Angeli's Marriage; The Strange Love-Making of Jimmy Dean!; James Dean's Black Madonna; Jimmy Dean: Why Parents Fear Him.* One hundred and ninety-eight such articles appeared in America alone during the two years following his death. Single issue fan magazines chased each other out onto the newsstands, and even a sports car journal climbed on the hearse: *James Dean's Last Ride – A Great Actor On the Road to Becoming a Greater Driver, When Death Released His Heavy Foot From the Throttle.* The New York shop girl who claimed to be in celestial communication with Dean sold half a million copies of her publication: *Jimmy Dean Returns! – Read his own words from the Beyond!*

Refusal to believe in his death had led to wild rumours that Dean was alive but so terribly disfigured that he had been shut away. Fans picketed the sanatoriums where they believed him to be. Other rumours had Dean escaping from the publicity he hated, having swapped identities with a dead Weutherich: he had entered a Buddhist monastery or the Roman Catholic church; he had, *pace* McCarthy, defected to Russia; he was hiding in downtown Los Angeles, tracking down his enemies with his switchblade and his gun; he would pay visits if girls left their photographs and addresses at a box number in a local newspaper.

There are still those who claim that the grave in Fairmount is empty: that Dean was not buried; or if he was buried, that his body was stolen by night soon after the funeral when the earth was still freshly dug. The intention had certainly been expressed, and the local police mounted a night and day guard on the cemetery for several weeks after the funeral. Later, when a memorial was put up to Dean outside the cemetery, the plinth was cut down and stolen.

A necrophagous cult was given a further unpleasant twist when Dean's smashed car was exhibited privately round Los Angeles. The Porsche had been bought from the wrecking yard by a sports car enthusiast, Dr William Eschrich, and cannibalised for spare parts from the relatively undamaged engine and gearbox (it was claimed that each car using any piece of the original Dean Porsche subsequently crashed). A young couple then bought the crumpled body shell from Dr Eschrich and exhibited it in a Los Angeles bowling alley: twenty-five cents to see Dean's crash car; fifty cents to sit in his death seat and touch the twisted, broken, blood-stained steering-wheel. They sold 800,000 tickets before they were persuaded, or coerced to stop the show. And still the death refused to die.

The car was broken up and sold for souvenirs. The Porsche began to take on the dimensions of a battleship as young Dean-worshippers bought up 'genuine' pieces of twisted aluminium, blood-stained seat fabric, even flakes of paint, and crushed glass.

Rings were sold with 'authentic' chips from his tombstone set like diamonds. Life-size James Dean heads were marketed in skin-texture 'Miracleflesh' at five dollars each. Three-inch moulded heads were manufactured based on a bust of Dean by Hollywood sculptor, Kenneth Kendall, the simulated stone model selling at $30, or alternative bronze editions at $150. The red *Rebel Without a Cause* zippered windcheaters retailed in a Hollywood store at $22.95, and were ordered for months afterwards. In Paris they became famous as the *blousons rouges*. 'If Jimmy were here and saw what was going on,' said Lew Bracker in an interview with *Life* magazine, 'he'd die all over again without the accident. It's mass hysteria. Somebody has paralysed the whole country. It's a creepy, almost a sick thing. It's something in Jimmy the teenagers saw, maybe themselves. Everybody mirrored themselves in Jimmy's fame and Jimmy's death.'

In the same *Life* article Nick Adams talked about letters he received from Dean fans: 'If you don't answer the letters you can't sleep at nights, they're such pleading letters. They ask me for anything Jimmy had, anything he came in contact with. They say, *send me anything Jimmy touched. If he touched a wall, send me a piece of the wall-paper.*'

Dean's New York apartment, and the house in San Fernando Valley, had been ransacked for souvenirs and mementoes. His friends managed to save very few of his personal possessions, and anyone who was known to have a piece of Dean memorabilia was liable to persecution. A girl asked Nick Adams for Dean's scrapbook: 'One night she tried to break into my house. I called the cops and they took her off. Another time she came back and pasted little signs all over my door. She put a burning wax triangle on my door, and a wax doll with the head burned off, and arms and legs, because I didn't give her the stuff.'

Adams claimed that he slept with loaded .32 and .45 automatics in the house, with his James Dean collection in a strongbox; and hourly police protection.

When the *Vampira* actress, Maila Nurmi, was accused in one magazine article of causing Dean's death by black magic, she was subjected to personal attacks by enraged Dean fans. And George Stevens received many letters threatening all kinds of dire consequences if he cut even one frame of Dean during the editing of *Giant*.

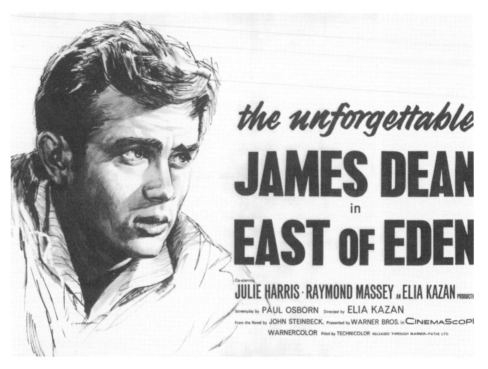

Warner Brothers took elaborate security precautions to prevent fans breaking into the studios for souvenirs. The 'wardrobe' pieces from the three films became prize items for collectors. The sculptor, Ken Kendall, still possesses one of Dean's pairs of Levi's from *Rebel Without a Cause*; the jacket worn for the fairground sequence in *East of Eden*, one of Cal's ties, a stand-up collar from *Giant* and Jett Rink's cummerbund that took Kendall fourteen years to track down.

In the absence of an official fan club many hundred of local organisations were set up all over the States, some of which were amalgamated to form the larger of the Dean fan clubs: 'Dedicated Deans' had a membership of 430,600; 'Dean's Teens' 392,450; 'Lest We Forget' 376,870; the 'James Dean Memorial Club' 328,590. Fan club membership in America totalled 3,800,000 paying members.

These fan clubs pressurised the awards organisations for posthumous recognition of Dean's acting career. James Dean was voted a Special Achievement medal by *Modern Screens*, Best Actor Award by the patrons of Motion Picture Exhibitors, World's Favourite Actor by the Hollywood Foreign Press Association, Best Performance of the Year by the Council of Motion Picture Organisations, Best Actor of 1955 by *Photoplay* magazine.

Only the Oscar finally eluded Dean. Nominated for his performances in both *East of Eden* and *Giant*, he was beaten on the first occasion (1955) by Ernest Borgnine in *Marty* and on the second occasion (1956) by Yul Brynner in *The King and I*.

Maila Nurmi later revealed that Dean had in fact received a pirate Oscar a few months before his death. It was a replica or an original stolen from Frank Sinatra, obtained by Maila Nurmi and Jack Simmons and presented by them to Dean with the engraving, 'to James Dean for the best performance in Googies 1955'.

Many of the fan clubs used to hold competitions to find the young man looking most like their dead hero. One winner of such a competition was put forward to play the part of James Dean when Warner Brothers started planning *The James Dean Story*, some time during 1956. It was eventually decided that the film should be a biographical documentary and an enormous amount of photographs, film clips and interviews were collected to illustrate the life and death of the actor. Robert Altman and George W. George were responsible for putting the film together, and various visual techniques were used to animate the photographs. Few of Dean's friends would agree to participate in the film and a sentimental commentary (written by script writer, Stewart Stern) ruined the overall effect. *The James Dean Story* was publicised as 'a different kind of motion picture', but when it was released in 1957 it failed at the box office and was ignored by the fans. Warners finally withdrew it from circulation (in the 1970s the film was acquired by an English company, VPS, and material from it used in a more serious and successful film biography by Ray Connolly).

The James Dean legend was given a semblance of dignity, when, a few months after his death, the citizens of Fairmount established a James Dean Memorial Foundation. The aims of the Foundation were the furtherance and patronage of the dramatic, musical and literary arts, with scholarships and facilities for study or performance. It seems the Foundation was set up in too much of a hurry, and never had adequate funds to promote much more than an occasional local theatrical show – though in more recent years royalties raised from the use of James Dean photographs in publicity campaigns have given Foundation work a more coherent financial framework. In those early years it was the example and memory of James Dean that gave most stimulus to local theatres, and more specifically to the aspirations of young Indiana actors. His drama coach, Adeline Nall, believed that Dean's short career remained a source of inspiration to her pupils in the Fairmount High School, and that one day the small mid-west town would produce another great American actor.

The inhabitants of Fairmount had taken great pride and pleasure in Dean's achievement: after *East of Eden* they had sent him a congratulatory scroll six feet long with signatures collected from all over Grant county; and in the week after his death the local paper produced a special commemorative issue. But their largely Quaker upbringing did not encourage the deification of dead heroes. Apart from the Memorial Foundation, and the fact that twenty-seven of the forty-eight boys born there in 1956 were called Jimmy, there was no local feeling to compare with the hysteria that had swept the rest of the continent. The town endured, with its characteristic hospitality, the curiosity of outsiders, hoping that the craze would eventually die away. The Winslow family had perforce to bear the brunt of that curiosity. Dean's uncle, Marcus Winslow: 'We kept hoping they'd leave it all alone, and leave the boy's memory to the people who really knew him for what he was – just an ordinary young man from a country home. Every time we thought it was finished it'd all start up again.'

Fairmount was in a sense submerged by the legend, literally so by the sheer number of people that flocked to the places where Dean had lived as a child and adolescent. One weekend afternoon in the autumn of 1956 the Winslows counted one hundred and eighty cars parked up and down the road outside the farm.

The small farming community may not have changed; but some of its identity must have been lost or confused when every out-of-State license-plate denoted another Dean pilgrimage.

The pilgrims came from all over the world. The cult had been taken up with particular fervour in Britain, France, Belgium, Germany, Italy, Finland, Poland, Greece, Japan, Indonesia, Iran, and most of Central and South America, as blue jeans and *blousons rouges* proliferated in the van of rock and roll.

The French awarded Dean a Crystal Star citation; the British an Academy Award. In Paris *Cinemonde* magazine dedicated every September issue for four years to the memory of James Dean, and thirteen out of seventeen critics on *Cahiers* voted *Rebel Without a Cause*

James Dean memorial service, October 1956, Fairmount.

A fan's shrine.

among the ten best films of the year. In London a Post Office van driver claimed to have seen *Rebel* four hundred times, and changed his name by deed poll to James Byron Dean. The English dramatist, Michael Hastings, wrote this preface to his play, *Don't Destroy Me*: 'This play is dedicated to the thought of James Dean. There is no other actor, and there never has been since the end of the war, who has so wholly represented my generation, here in England; but strangely he is American. This play, in its entirety, I give to Dean. But he is dead now.'

A portrait of Dean even appeared in the summer exhibition at the Royal Academy in London, when, in 1957, they hung John Minton's picture of James Dean next to Annigoni's Duke of Edinburgh – John Minton had committed suicide only a few months before.

There were clubs in Germany where girls would give themselves unconditionally to any boy who looked like their dead idol. Two Hamburg girls killed themselves in 1959, saying that life without him was unbearable. In Poland James Dean became a symbol of protest against the Communist hierarchy; in Italy and South America a protest against Catholicism. Everywhere he was a focus – or more often than not a journalistic excuse – for discontent, unhappiness, self-pity or violence. John Dos Passos wrote in *Esquire* magazine in 1958:

> There is nothing much deader than a dead motion picture actor,
> and yet,
> even after James Dean had been some years dead,
> When they filed out of the close darkness and the breathed-out
> air of the second and third and fourth run motion picture theatres
> where they'd been seeing James Dean's old films, they still lined up:
> the boys in the jackboots and the leather jackets, the boys in
> the skin-tight jeans, the boys in broad motorbike belts,
> before the mirrors in the restroom

to look at themselves
and see
James Dean;
the resentful hair
the deep eyes floating in lonesomeness,
the bitter beat look
the scorn on the lip
Their pocket combs were out; they tousled up their hair and patted it down just so;
made big eyes at their eyes in the mirror
pouted their lips in a sneer
the lost cats in love with themselves
just like James Dean.

It is impossible to judge whether the impact of the Dean legend would have been as great had it come at any other time. He had become the first idol and symbol for a young generation beginning to define an identity of its own. He had given young people self-awareness, a degree of self-pity and self-indulgence, above all a style of anger, at a time when they were rejecting the values of the society around them.

'After the Second World War there was a very understandable and correct disgust felt by the younger generation for the generation that had caused the war,' said Elia Kazan. 'There was a genuine feeling that the moral standards of the old generation were hollow, that they no longer meant anything and weren't valid for us any more. So there was a very genuine questioning of the values of their parents by the young people.'

The James Dean generation had been dominated by the leaden atmosphere of Eisenhower paternalism: obedience was still a habit; a shooting war in Korea had reinforced wartime myths; and Cold War had been moved beyond the confines of Berlin or occupied Europe, across the Atlantic, where Americans submitted with surprisingly little protest to the inquisition of the anti-Communist witch-hunts. For young people discontent, restlessness, or even mere self-expression were undefined beyond a general unease with the post-depression and post-war materialism of their parents. Echoes of wartime violence fed fantasy in the cinemas, while outside all was anti-climax. And over everything loomed the nuclear mushroom cloud – at the end of all roads. Such a confusion had produced a state of mind not dissimilar to the post-Vietnam numbness of the 1970s after the comparative failure of a decade of protest, the triumph of corruption, greed and political brutality around the world.

Then, as now, youth found little or no identification with traditional heroes. The new-style hero in the 1950s was the violent or troubled outsider: Brando in *The Wild One* ('My old man hit harder than that'); Montgomery Clift in *From Here to Eternity* ('If a man don't go his own way he's nothing'); and, in another field, the 'cool' despair of Holden Caulfield in *The Catcher in the Rye* ('Anyway, I'm sort of glad they've got the atomic bomb invented. If there's ever another war, I'm going to sit right the hell on top of it. I'll volunteer for it, I swear to God I will').

James Dean seemed to personify them all. His troubled, sometimes violent vulnerability was instantly identified by his own generation. As an alienated rebel hero Dean expressed the full confusion of emotions: 'The bewilderment, disgust, and half-stifled directionless good of mishandled adolescence' wrote the *Times Educational Supplement* about *Rebel Without a Cause*; the anguish; the burst of *joie de vivre* and confidence; the eternal questioning; the demand for honesty, truth and direct behaviour; the growing and painful awareness that all was not possible.

The English critic Derek Prouse described in *Sight and Sound* Dean's rebel without a cause:

The eyes withdrawn and undeceived; the inflexions at once relaxed and bitter in denial of all expectation; the awkward grace of youth and the moments of eruptive conviction that somewhere, something is hideously wrong outside himself. Drawn equally to the life of his own generation and to a superior instinctual world of the spirit, he drifts – recoiling on the one hand from the cruelties of other adolescents, and on the other from the stifling claims of his parents. The actor movingly captures the conflict in all its multiple evasions, betrayals, sudden giggling release of tension, and agonised deadlock, and achieves a genuinely poetic account of a modern misfit.

This portrait of alienated youth was not confined to the Anglo-Saxon worlds of Britain and America. In Paris François Truffaut wrote in the magazine *Arts* one year after Dean's death:

> In James Dean today's youth discovers itself. Less for the reasons usually advanced – violence, sadism, hysteria, pessimism, cruelty, and filth – than for others infinitely more simple and commonplace: modesty of feeling; continual fantasy life; moral purity, without relation to everyday morality but all the more rigorous; eternal adolescent love of tests and trials; intoxication, pride, and regret at feeling oneself 'outside' society; refusal and desire to become integrated; and finally acceptance, or refusal, of the world as it is.

If other generations continue still to find him, it is for much the same reasons. The identification was never, as traditionally with a film star, the fantasy 'how nice to be like that'; it was instead the conviction 'that is how I am'. And the conviction could only be strengthened with the discovery that Dean lived and died the reality of his screen image. It is perhaps this authenticity that has held the image of James Dean an unlikely survivor through four decades of intense political and social change.

The year following Dean's death became for various reasons a watershed in the post-war way of life. In December 1955, in Montgomery, Alabama, Mrs Rosa Parks refused to give up her seat on a bus to a white man and sparked off the first public boycott in the fight for racial equality. In Europe John Osborne's Jimmy Porter arrived on the London stage in *Look Back in Anger*, as Britain and France embarked on their last and disastrous imperial adventure along the Suez Canal. In Hungary the barricades went up on the streets of Budapest to challenge, however hopelessly, the totalitarian dominance of Rakosi's secret police and the Russian tanks. The years of protest and direct action had begun, and young people all over the world began to find articulate expression for their rebellion.

Even the non-political world of the teenage consumer was living its own revolution. The generation that had found its first identity and style in the James Dean films was discovering the excitement of a sub-culture of music as rock 'n' roll finally broke into the hit parades all over the world. While the James Dean audience remained, focused upon the receding image of their dead hero, Bill Haley and Elvis Presley arrived on radio, the live stage, the screen, and in the record shops, to claim them. The newcomers should have killed a dead legend and yet the James Dean image remained a perpetual backcloth to the early decades of pop-culture. As a screen image, as a popular idol, or as a mythological hero, James Dean marked his and subsequent generations, and there was scarcely a film star or pop star in those years who had not absorbed or been absorbed by the James Dean trauma.

Elvis Presley was the contemporary, four years younger than Dean, who arrived in Hollywood one year after Dean's death to make his own film debut in *Love Me Tender*. The first of Presley's hit singles, 'Heartbreak Hotel', had been released only a few months previously, and his fast transition to the screen was certainly influenced by the Hollywood search for a new young star to replace James Dean. When Presley met Nick Ray in one of the studio canteens, he acknowledged, with a salaam, the director of a James Dean movie and proceeded to recite whole scenes of dialogue from *Rebel Without a Cause*. The one journalist's tag he apparently accepted with honour was the title of 'rock 'n' roll' James Dean', though his producer on *Love Me Tender*, David Weisbart (Ray's producer on *Rebel*), denied any real similarity between the two stars. He compared the two of them in an interview with Joe Hyams of the *Herald Tribune*:

> So far as teenagers are concerned Elvis is what I call a safety valve. By that I mean they scream, holler, articulate, and let go of their emotions when they see him perform. But when they watched Jimmy perform they bottled their emotions and were sort of sullen and brooding. Elvis is completely outgoing, whereas Jimmy was the direct opposite. Basically, Jimmy was a loner, whereas Elvis is gregarious.

Inevitably the cinema tried to produce its James Dean substitutes. Anthony Perkins, Dean Stockwell, Warren Beatty, Jean Paul Belmondo (as later Martin Sheen, Johnny Depp or the short-lived River Phoenix) were among the unfortunates hailed as his successors, though there was only one screen performance to resemble Dean at all closely in image and in acting style, Zbigniew Cybulski's haunting portrayal of the doubting young partisan, Maciek, in Wajda's Polish war film *Ashes and Diamonds*.

Whatever may have been achieved in similar acting styles a 'replica' of James Dean was not really relevant to the films of the late 50s and 60s. Rebellion was becoming socially and politically orientated, articulate in music and words. And 'rebellion' on the screen was increasingly concerned either with the harsh and uncompromising expression of an amoral truth in violence (Marlon Brando in *One Eyed Jacks*, Steve McQueen in *Hell is for Heroes*, Lee Marvin in *Point Blank*); or with the dissociated anarchy of the misfit or outsider – which might well have become Dean's territory (Paul Newman in *The Hustler*, Kirk Douglas in *Lonely are the Brave*, Jean Pierre Leaud in *The 400 Blows*, Charles Aznavour in *Shoot the Pianist*, Newman and Robert Redford in *Butch Cassidy*, Warren Beatty in *Bonnie and Clyde*, Jack Nicholson, Peter Fonda and Dennis Hopper in *Easy Rider*, Malcolm McDowell in *If....* and *A Clockwork Orange*).

Perhaps in the evolution of the pop superstars one could draw a spurious link between Dean and the blunt suggestiveness of Presley or Jerry Lee Lewis; the adolescent hesitations of Buddy Holly; the plaintiveness of the Everly Brothers; the violence of Little Richard; the androgyny of David Bowie; the sensuality of Mick Jagger; the inventive, anarchic genius of Jimi Hendrix. But although James Dean had some influence on the manner and style of pop, his survival as a cult figure had far more to do with the validity, and therefore the permanence, of his general mood, the image of adolescent revolt and self-assertion.

In this context the one parallel immediately apparent is between Dean and Bob Dylan, who also came, at a younger age (he was six years junior to Presley) from a James Dean adolescence.

'We used to go to all the James Dean shows those couple of years after he died,' said Hoikkala (drummer in Dylan's first group, The Golden Chords). 'We'd go down to the news-stand and get all the magazines that had any articles at all on Dean. We idolised him both as a person and an actor. We felt, including Bob, that his acting was actually himself. He wasn't just acting the roles he was in. The roles were him.'

Dylan's own style of dress and behaviour was heavily influenced by that adolescent identity with Dean. The Dean image was there, on the record sleeve of *The Freewheeling Bob Dylan*, with Dylan bowed and hunched up, arm in arm with Suze Rotolo, scuffing through the snow on West Fourth Street.

Dylan was singing for the new rebellion, creating the articulate poetry of protest or reality, his image and sound dominating the 1960s, as Dean had dominated the mid-1950s. And it was Dylan who nearly died on his motorbike, breaking his neck in an accident that might, in the event of his death, have eclipsed the Dean legend.

'He had the same kind of magnetism as James Dean,' said Jack Elliot. 'Dean was the first cat I ever met with that kind of thing, the magnetism and the feeling he was running too fast. And Bob was the second.'

Like Dean, Dylan's life became obsessive in its search for meaningful expression; and like the qualities in Dean's acting, his songs express simultaneously the smile and the sneer, that mocking, melancholy lyricism of a perpetual outsider.

A decade later James Dean lived again in the songs and folklore of the 70s. In 1971 Don McLean linked him with the superstars in his lament 'American Pie'; Dylan the Jester, Presley the King, Joan Baez the Queen:

> When the Jester sang for the King and Queen
> in a coat he'd borrowed from James Dean
> and a voice that came from you and me.

In 1973 the *New Musical Express* devoted a centre page to a James Dean article by Roy Carr and Nick Kent, acknowledging the revival of what they termed a James Dean fetish. And in 1974 David Essex sang ambiguously of the myth image in his song 'Rock On':

> Still looking for that blue jean baby queen,
> prettiest girl I've ever seen
> see her shake on the movie screen
> Jimmy Dean – James Dean.

In 1976 a musical, *James Dean* (Robert Campbell and John Howlett), ran for five weeks in London's West End, subsequently to become a regular production with the Japanese women's theatre, the Takar Azuka Revue Troupe; the celebration of Dean, acted by a girl, becoming the ultimate androgynous idol. And now in the mid-90s, forty years after his death, a feature film, *James Dean – Race With Destiny* is in production with Casper Van Dien as the title role.

Jim, Jimmy, James Dean. The name is familiar, though the kids are not too sure about him – was he a folk singer, a racing driver, a superstar? It does not matter to them. They know he is a hero. In the words of Roy Carr and Nick Kent:

> It really is the case that more often than not, the only heroes that you can really trust are the dead ones. Are you there James Dean? Knock once for Yes, twice for No.

10. The Doomed Outsider

> I know I want to be an actor but that isn't it.
> That's not all. Just being an actor or a director,
> even a good one, isn't enough. There's got to
> be something more than just that.
>
> *James Dean*

JAMES DEAN was, as perhaps any great actor must be, the overwhelming consciousness of self in search of identity. He existed at whatever level or levels he found himself; he exists at whatever level or levels you find him: rebel, mythological hero, vulnerable child, ghoul, beautiful victim, monster, gay icon, sexual predator, sexual victim, self-destructive perfectionist, living legend, dead legend. Ambiguity is inevitable, initiated by the real contradictions in Dean's personality, helped on its way by the stories, exaggerated, apocryphal, sensationalised, that gather round the myth.

Studio publicists have left us the marginalia: his favourite Hollywood restaurant was the Villa Capri; his favourite beer, Guinness or Tuborg; his favourite piece of music, Mozart's *Eine Kleine Nachtmusik*; his favourite non-four-letter adjective, 'crocko', denoting something or someone false, pointless, or bad. On two and four wheels he owned, at various times, the 'Whizzer', a BSA, a Lancia motorscooter, several twin cylinder Triumphs, a 1939 Chevrolet, an MG TA, a Porsche Spyder, a Ford Station Wagon, a lightweight competition Porsche. He possessed extensive hi-fi equipment; a Leica camera; a Rollicord, and a turret-lens Bolex movie camera.

However, almost everything else about him is controversial. Even his physical statistics are questioned: he was five foot seven, eight, ten inches tall; he weighed a hundred and forty-five, fifty, fifty-five pounds; his hair was dirty blond, brown, straw-coloured; his eyes were blue, green, grey. If you look at him on screen you are not quite sure what you have seen. The proportions are slightly wrong: his legs stocky and short; his eyes too close, deep-set, and out of line, giving him in frontal close-up, something of a squint. It was a defect he would instinctively try to correct in poses, by dropping his head into one hand and levering up the low eyebrow.

The look is twisted, suggesting the 'spastic' or the 'cripple' that Kazan described. And for many people his personality remained associated with that twisted image – selfish and ruthless, a difficult colleague and even more difficult friend.

Nicholas Ray called Dean 'the most clear-thinking, non-neurotic, and non-psychotic actor' he had ever worked with, yet even Ray admits an area of difficulty he found impossible to overcome. 'Between belief and action lay the obstacle of Jimmy's own deep

Having fun at a Hollywood party during shooting of Rebel.

obscure uncertainty. Disappointed or unsatisfied he was the child who goes to his private corner and refuses to speak.' He was in his own life, as on screen, the Jim Stark who declared so emphatically, 'I want answers *now*!'

Bill Bast's mother once spent a whole day alone with Dean in the Santa Monica penthouse he was sharing with her son. When Bast returned home in the evening he found his mother in tears and close to hysteria. Dean, in the middle of some mood or tantrum, had not said a word all day. 'It was like being locked up with a dead man,' she said. Dean himself was either unaware, or unrepentant of the distress he had caused.

Mood, mischief or malice? Even on the set of *Rebel*, the happiest of his three pictures, Dean could pull some nasty tricks. Nick Ray remembers him teasing Natalie Wood: 'He would try and break her up if he was playing off-camera. He sometimes made her cry, and we'd have to yell at him "Jimmy, get your ass off-stage".' Yet Natalie Wood remembers him as an easy actor to work with, creative, co-operative, very confident, and not at all protective or paranoiac. After *Rebel* he even apologised to her for what he considered had been a lack of concentration during his final week of shooting – a time when he was already preparing for his role in *Giant*.

Professional dedication and personal insecurity were the inseparable characteristics of his behaviour off-set. Kazan likened him to a fretful or uncertain animal: 'With affection, understanding and patience, he got awfully good. God, he gave everything he had. There wasn't anything he held back.'

The force of his acting, and the nature of his success certainly presupposes some element of opportunism, ruthlessness, and above all, aggression. Dennis Hopper called him 'the first guerrilla artist ever to work in movies', and recalls that once on a set 'Jimmy pulled a switchblade on the director and threatened at arms' length that he would kill him if he didn't allow him to play that particular scene the way he wanted.'

It is Dennis Hopper again who tells the story, hearsay since he was not himself present, of Dean's introduction to the unit on *East of Eden*. Crew and cast are gathered together while Elia Kazan gives them a little introduction: 'This boy may not seem much, but he's going to be pure gold on screen.' Then a door opens and Dean comes through, yelling at them all with his hand jerking up and down in the appropriate two-fingered gesture: 'Fuck you, fuck you, fuck you, fuck you.'

Dennis Hopper found the story symbolic of Dean's challenge to establishment attitudes: 'When you're a young actor in Hollywood everyone comes up to you and lets you know how James Cagney played that scene in 1930 and how Humphrey Bogart did it in 1940 – Dean just eliminated all of that in one gesture.'

These incidents were symptomatic of the apparently irresistible urge Dean possessed to move to extremes; to create outrage. One part of such behaviour was certainly exhibitionist. He was always watching people out of the corner of an eye, to note the effect of moments of outrageous or unconventional behaviour. But he also had that need for adrenalin, the deliberate testing of himself and his audience to see just how far he could reach, both as an actor and as a person. It is a dangerous process, and one that Lee Strasberg had noticed back in Dean's New York days: 'His behaviour and

Happy days on the set of Rebel.

personality seemed to be part of a pattern which invariably had to lead to something destructive. I always had a strange feeling that there was in Jimmy a sort of doomed quality.'

James Dean never had detachment, objectivity, or caution in which to take refuge. Whatever he did, idiotic, bizarre, unpleasant, unkind, he would do with conviction. His lack of pretence was an essential quality of his acting. It gave him authenticity. But it presupposed a refusal to compromise, an arrogance, that he applied with near disastrous effects in his day-to-day life.

Sal Mineo recalls an incident during the shooting on *Rebel* when he, Natalie Wood, and Dean were called up into the front office to have their costumes checked by Jack Warner. They were in a reception room, and Dean was lying on the floor with his feet stuck out through the door into the corridor. 'One of the senior producers or executives walked by and said, "What the hell do you think you're doing? Get up off the floor and get your feet out of the hallway." And Jimmy looked up at him and didn't even move, and he said very loudly and clearly, "Fuck you." And this guy looked at him and said, "How dare you talk

'I always had a strange feeling that there was in Jimmy a sort of doomed quality.'

to me like that," and he sort of rushed away. Within three minutes the whole place was ablaze, people running around, and the secretary in tears. Then another big-shot came along: "Do you realise who you talked to?" Jimmy said, "No. And I don't give a shit. Who the fuck is he to come on so strong with me?"'

The identity of his motivation was never clear: was he the orphan of an ambitious mother for whom he had an obligation to succeed? Bill Bast's 'lonely shepherd'? The 'stray animal looking for a home' that Dennis Stock had described? Until acting possessed him, Dean's life and ambitions had been expressed in conventional terms: the model high school student; the successful sportsman; the average country boy, helping when he had to on the farm. If anything set him apart from his contemporaries it was only the passion of his dedication to whatever task he had in hand. When he discovered the potential of his own self-expression, the passion, whatever its origin, drove him to any extreme he considered necessary in order to fulfil his potential.

Whatever experience was lacking to him in his own life he deliberately set out to acquire. He once met a girl who had recently lost her leg in a road accident. He asked her all about it, how it had happened, what it had felt like, what she was thinking when she didn't know if she was going to lose it or not. The sculptor, Kenneth Kendall, remembers the girl accompanying Dean on a visit to him, and talking about her accident: 'Dean was listening to her with a quite extraordinary intensity, hitting himself at each grisly detail, and muttering – "Shit, oh shit."' Dean later took the girl back to her room: 'We went up to my place because he wanted to see it. Then he wanted to touch it. He asked me everything

164

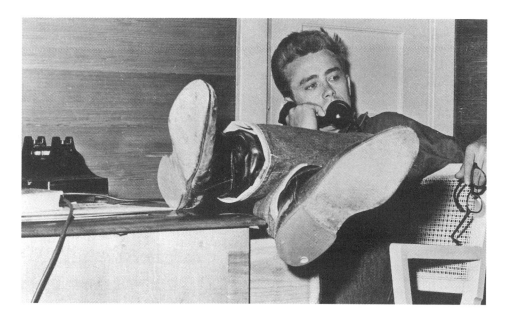

In the office at Warner Brothers (above); and with his Bolex movie camera (below).

Clowning around in the RCA building.

about it, how it made me feel, how it changed my way of thinking and living, how I learnt to walk without it. We talked for hours just about my leg. We even laughed about it at the end. Then he just got up and went away.'

It is a disturbing, uncomfortable picture; macabre; obsessive; sick; or just the desire to know, the need to share experience?

If there was one characteristic that seemed to govern his life it was this determination to know and experience everything. An intensity of purpose drove him like a puritan conscience; and it was often a very naive intensity. His lack of learning and knowledge annoyed him. During early days at college he used to carry a dictionary around with him, plagued by high-powered conversations that he could not understand. He would always search out the people he could use as teachers or counsellors. Bill Bast had watched the process at work: 'He sapped the minds of his friends as a bloodsucker saps the strength of an unsuspecting man. Almost fanatically he approached each person he met, whether prominent or obscure, with the same attitude: "I will draw from him all he knows."'

One of his friends and teachers, the composer Len Rosenman, believes that much of Dean's intellectual insecurity stemmed from an apparent dyslexic difficulty he had in reading; though it is not clear whether the problem was with the actual reading, or whether he found complex subject-matter hard to assimilate. The only time Rosenman tried to discuss the subject with him, Dean stormed off in a huff.

He certainly suffered an impatience to master everything quickly and with the minimum of effort. Rosenman taught him the rudiments of playing the piano and found him a good but lazy student. He was musical and reasonably talented but he could never really understand why it was not possible to play the major works of Beethoven and Mozart without years of study and practice.

During the last weeks of his life, Pegot Waring was teaching him to model in clay, and she also found his naive impatience difficult to cope with: 'He wanted to know just about every single fact, idea, and theory, that had been discovered by man clear back to the stone age.'

His ambitions beyond acting were wild and he had absolute faith that he would soon accomplish them all; directing films; writing; carving giant sculptures; becoming a Grand Prix racing driver. George Stevens later described the force of Dean's motivation: 'He was a disturbed boy tremendously dedicated to some intangible beacon of his own, and neither he nor anyone else might ever know what it was.'

He applied a similar explorative intensity to his personal relationships. He would approach everyone with an urgent probing curiosity, and an opportunist's eye for the people who could help him. But he also had an extraordinary and uncomfortable sensitivity. He once met two friends of Nick Ray, Michael and Connie Bessie, a married couple Ray had known for many years: 'After I had introduced them to Jimmy, Connie sat down on the couch. There was a cushion beside her. With an unconscious, mechanical gesture she picked it up and cradled it in her lap. Jimmy watched her. After a moment he asked, very intent and quiet: "Can't you have a child of your own?" She was speechless. She left the room, and I went out after her. She was almost crying, not out of self-pity, but profoundly moved by the perception. She and her husband had just adopted a baby.'

But it was a sensitivity that contrasted with Dean's mistrust of love, or even of close friendship, a result perhaps of the early loss of that solitary and very dependent relationship with his mother. He would drift, seemingly free, casual and independent, in, out and around the lives of his friends or relatives. But the freedom was illusory. He was alone, but he needed people, and when he felt threatened he would hold tight to a relationship, demanding more from it than he could emotionally cope with. Mistrust and need were never apparently reconciled and, as Kazan had occasion to observe, 'Jimmy made life hell for any girl who gave him affection.' 'Do you love me?' he would continue to ask each male or female friend. 'Do you love me?'

Some such insecurity lies within most of us to varying degrees. Dean turned his vulnerability into an art form.

Relating to people – spiritually, cerebrally, maternally, fraternally, however one defines it – was probably more difficult and therefore more important to him than physical relations. Whatever his appetites, he does not appear to have found the availability or execution of sex difficult; nor did it seem to play a particularly important part in his life. He was occasionally boastful about it in an adolescent fashion, referring to his women in the early days as 'conquests', in later days as 'clitori'. He was certainly bisexual – a close friend, Jonathan Gilmore, referred to him as 'multisexual' – though how actively heterosexual or homosexual no one really knows. More men than women claim to have slept with him; but when Bill Bast drew up a list of the homosexuals who insisted that, at one time or another Dean had lived with them, he calculated Dean would have had to have lived over a hundred years to have fulfilled all their claims. The sensuality of his acting was more feminine, like the melancholy narcissism of a male flamenco dancer. But his audience related to his physical image and attraction in equal proportion, male and female.

Had he been a contemporary superstar there would be less mystery: Freddie Mercury, Elton John or David Bowie live or lived their lives without that same

prurient speculation over their sexuality, largely because they felt no need to hide it. Dean instead lived in an age of taboos when adultery or extra-marital sex were forbidden subjects of public conversation; and homosexuality an evil identified with drugs and Communism. Speculation about his sex life is only marginally relevant, insofar as his drive in that direction was or was not sublimated elsewhere. Otherwise it is mere curiosity, and unfortunately much of the gossip and sensationalism about his life was motivated by just that curiosity. Queens and starlets grabbed at instant kudos with their revelations. Royston Ellis, in his biography *Rebel*, called Dean a 'bisexual psychopath', and the fictionalised accounts of Dean's life, unpleasant and distasteful in their spurious suggestion of an approximation to facts, depended for much of their glamour on the controversial sexual behaviour of their Dean-like heroes, John Preston (*The Immortal* by Walter Ross), and John Calvin Lewis (*Farewell My Slightly Tarnished Hero* by Edwin Corley). Character assassination was the order of the day as photographs were circulated of a very hazily defined young man said to be Dean, sitting naked in a tree, playing with a large erection (Donald Spoto discovered the young man to have been a mentally retarded boy set up by his cousin as a James Dean look-alike).

Does his sexuality matter? If you're a woman, you'd probably rather he was heterosexual or bisexual; if you're a man, the bisexuality may or may not trouble or excite you; if you're gay, his homosexuality could be important to you. But the heart and soul that fuelled his extraordinary ability to communicate mood and emotion came from somewhere far deeper than mere sexual confusion. At 24 he'd barely have matured out of a normal bisexuality of youth and young manhood.

As for where his instincts and emotions might have subsequently taken him, he empathised with the softness and gentleness and warmth of the women he knew; he dreamed of creating the family unit he'd lost as a young boy. Given a normal lifespan he'd probably have created a family or two of his own – but would almost certainly have continued to explore the ambiguous and androgynous sensuality that was the life-blood of his physical consciousness.

Dennis Hopper in his recent introduction to *James Dean – Behind The Scene* is adamant:

James Dean was not gay. The two great loves of his life in Hollywood were Pier Angeli and Ursula Andress. Pier Angeli married Vic Damone. James Dean sat on his motorbike outside the church. She'd asked Jimmy to marry her. He'd asked her to wait until he saw how his career was going. Ursula Andress met John Derek and proceeded to parade him on the set of *Giant* after Jimmy refused to marry her for the same reason.

Rogers Brackett and Jonathan Gilmour would have been equally adamant – that at the very least Dean was actively bisexual.

When *The James Dean Story* opened in London two years after his death, *The Times* described Dean as:

A lonely young man, haunted by insecurity, longing for affection, yet thrusting it away from him, gifted yet suspecting his gifts, ambitious yet preferring to live like a tramp, in love, like T. E. Lawrence, with speed, and hugging a surly manner around him like a protecting cloak.

Chris White described Dean to Val Holley as the boy with 'a leak in his heart'; another New York friend from the Iroquois, David Diamond, called him 'the loneliest person I ever knew'; Edgar Morin defined him as 'the perfect mythological hero'. Dean was orphan and lone wolf, rejected and rejecting in love; a misfit seeking his own destiny; a doomed hero meeting death in his search for the absolute; and, after death, the immortal whose death could not be accepted.

Dean's rebellion was aggressive and uncompromising, but inarticulate beyond a general anger. It was as directionless as the violence of a street delinquent and yet it captured the imagination of a generation as universally as Bob Dylan's more specific rebellion a decade later. Perhaps because there was no impediment to identification. Dean was not a superman fighting with guns; not even, on screen, with motorcycles. He was as Dylan, 'Average common too ... just like him and the same as you ... everybody's brother and son.' The truth in his rebellion was the bafflement, the reluctance actually to rebel, the puzzled interrogative, the bewilderment of anger. Whether it came from his acting or derived from him as a person, his central expression was a quality of sadness, and in certain moods at certain times people will choose before anything else the truthful portrayal of pain or despair.

Dean's screen image was created from, fed, and finally destroyed by his own despairing pursuit of whatever loss and undefined vision had been haunting him since childhood. An ever-receding vision, but one he always believed he would one day capture and understand. Perhaps vision and reality finally coincided for the briefest possible moment at that country intersection, westbound on Highway 466.

Filmography

Radio

Bit parts in:
CBS Radio Workshop
Alias Jane Doe
Stars Over Hollywood
Sam Spade

Television

1951
Pepsi Cola commercial
Hill Number One
Beat the Clock (stand-by work)

1952
US Steel Hour – Prologue to Glory
Bit parts in unspecified episodes of:
Tales of Tomorrow
Treasury-Men in Action
Martin Kane
Campbell Sound Stage
Danger
Kraft Theatre

1953
Kate Smith Hour – 'Hound of Heaven'
Treasury-Men in Action – 'The Case of the Watchful Dog'
Treasury-Men in Action – 'The Case of the Sawed-Off Shotgun'
Campbell Sound Stage – 'Something for an Empty Briefcase'

Campbell Sound Stage – 'Life Sentence'
Kraft Theatre – 'Keep Our Honor Bright'
Kraft Theatre – 'A Long Time Till Dawn'
Danger – 'No Room'
Danger – 'The Little Woman'
Danger – 'Death is My Neighbor'
US Steel Hour – 'The Thief'
Studio One Summer Theatre – 'Sentence of Death'
Omnibus
Johnson's Wax Program – Robert Montgomery Presents 'Harvest'

1954
General Electric Theatre – 'I Am a Fool'
General Electric Theatre – 'The Dark, Dark Hours'
Danger – 'Padlocks'
Philco TV Playhouse – 'Run Like a Thief'

1955
Schlitz Playhouse – 'The Unlighted Road'
Interviewed on Lever Brothers' *Lux Video Theater* for the *East of Eden* preview
Colgate Variety Hour – Award presented posthumously by *Modern Screen* on its twenty-fifth anniversary

1956
Steve Allen Show. A tribute

1957
A tribute to Dean on CBS
'The James Dean Legend' produced by Associated Rediffusion, England

Theatre

SEE THE JAGUAR
Play in three acts by N. Richard Nash
Produced by Lemuel Ayers in association with Helen Jacobson
Directed by Michael Gordon

Cast: Philip Pine *(Hilltop)*, David Clarke *(Yetter)*, Constance Ford *(Janna)*, Roy Fant *(Grampa Ricks)*, Margaret Baker *(Mrs Wilkins)*, Arthur Kennedy *(Dave Ricks)*, Cameron Prud'Homme *(Brad)*, George Tyne *(Harvey)*, Arthur Batanides *(Frank)*, Ted Jacques *(Meeker)*, Florence Sundstrom *(Mrs Meeker)*, James Dean *(Wally Wilkins)*, Dane Knell *(Jee Jee)*, Harrison Dowd *(Sam)*, Harry Bergman *(Andy)*, Tony Kraber *(Carson)*
Premiere 3 December 1952 at the Cort Theater

THE IMMORALIST
Play in three acts by Ruth and Augustus Goetz
Based on a novel by André Gide
Produced by Billy Rose
Directed by Daniel Mann

Cast: Geraldine Page *(Marcelline)*, John Heldabrand *(Dr Robert)*, Charles Dingle *(Bocage)*, Louis Jordan *(Michael)*, James Dean *(Bachir)*, Paul Huber *(Dr Garrin)*, Adelaide Klein *(Sidma)*, David J. Stewart *(Moktir)*, Billy Gunn *(Dolit)*
Premiere 1 February 1954 at the Royale Theater

Film

James Dean played minor roles in *Sailor Beware, Fixed Bayonets,* and *Has Anybody Seen My Gal?* His three major roles were in *East of Eden, Rebel Without a Cause* and *Giant.*

SAILOR BEWARE (1951)
With Dean Martin, Jerry Lewis, Corrinne Calvert, Marion Marshall
Directed by Hal Walker

FIXED BAYONETS (1951)
With Richard Basehart, Gene Evans, Michael O'Shea, Richard Hylton
Directed by Samuel Fuller

HAS ANYBODY SEEN MY GAL? (1952)
With Charles Coburn, Rock Hudson, Piper Laurie, Lynn Bari, William Reynolds
Directed by Douglas Sirk

EAST OF EDEN (1955)
Produced and Directed by Elia Kazan
Screenplay by Paul Osborn, based on the novel by John Steinbeck
Music by Leonard Rosenman
Director of Photography: Ted McCord
Art Directors: James Basevi, Malcolm Bert
Edited by Owen Marks

Cast: James Dean *(Cal Trask)*, Julie Harris *(Abra)*, Raymond Massey *(Adam Trask)*, Richard Davalos *(Aron Trask)*, Burl Ives *(Sam, the Sheriff)*, Jo Van Fleet *(Kate)*, Albert Dekker *(Will Hamilton)*, Lois Smith *(Anne)*, Harold Gordon *(Mr Albrecht)*, Richard Garrick *(Dr Edwards)*, Timothy Carey *(Joe)*, Nick Dennis *(Rantani)*, Lonny Chapman *(Roy)*, Barbara Baxley *(Nurse)*, Bette Treadville *(Barmaid)*, Tex Mooney *(Bartender)*, Harry Cording *(Bouncer)*, Loretta Rush *(Card Dealer)*, Bill Phillips *(Coalman)*, Mario Siletti *(Piscora)*, Jonathan Haze *(Piscora's Son)*, Jack Carr, Roger Creed, Effie Laird, Wheaton Chambers, Ed Clark, Al Ferguson, Franklyn Farnum, Rose Plummer *(Carnival People)*, John George *(Photographer)*, C. Ramsay Hill *(English Officer)*, Edward McNally *(Soldier)*, Earle Hodgins *(Shooting Gallery Attendant)*
Cinemascope Warner Color 115 minutes
Shot during May–August 1954
Premiered in the USA on 9 April 1955

REBEL WITHOUT A CAUSE (1955)
Directed by Nicholas Ray
Screenplay by Stewart Stern from an adaptation by Irving Shulman of a story by Nicholas Ray
Produced by David Weisbart
Music by Leonard Rosenman

Director of Photography: Ernest Haller
Art Director: Malcolm Bert
Edited by William Ziegler

Cast: James Dean *(Jim Stark)*, Natalie Wood *(Judy)*, Sal Mineo *(Plato)*, Jim Backus *(Jim's Father)*, Ann Doran *(Jim's Mother)*, Corey Allen *(Buzz)*, William Hopper *(Judy's Father)*, Rochelle Hudson *(Judy's Mother)*, Virginia Brissac *(Jim's Grandma)*, Nick Adams *(Moose)*, Dennis Hopper *(Goon)*, Jack Simmons *(Cookie)*, Marietta Canty *(Plato's Maid)*, Jack Grinnage *(Chick)*, Beverly Long *(Helen)*, Steffi Sidney *(Mil)*, Frank Mazzola *(Crunch)*, Tom Bernard *(Harry)*, Clifford Morris *(Cliff)*, Ian Wolfe *(Lecturer)*, Edward Platt *(Juvenile Officer Ray)*, Robert Foulk *(Gene)*, Jimmy Baird *(Bean)*, Dick Wessel *(Guide)*, Nelson Leigh *(Sergeant)*, Dorothy Abbot *(Nurse)*, Louise Lane *(Woman Officer)*, House Peters *(Officer)*, Gus Schilling *(Attendant)*, Bruce Noonan *(Monitor)*, Almira Sessions *(Old Lady Teacher)*, Peter Miller *(Hoodlum)*, Paul Bryar *(Desk Sergeant)*, Paul Birch *(Police Chief)*, Robert Williams *(Moose's Father)*, David McMahon *(Crunch's Father)*
Cinemascope Warner Color 111 minutes (USA) 106 minutes (UK) as knife fight originally censored
Shot during March–May 1955
Premiered in the USA on 29 October 1955

GIANT (1956)
Directed by George Stevens
Screenplay by Fred Guiol and Ivan Moffat from the novel by Edna Ferber
Produced by Henry Ginsberg and George Stevens
Music by Dimitri Tiomkin
Director of Photography: William C. Mellor
Art Director: Ralph Hurst
Edited by Fred Bohaman and Phil Anderson
Cast: Elizabeth Taylor *(Leslie Lynton Benedict)*, Rock Hudson *(Bick Benedict)*, James Dean *(Jett Rink)*, Mercedes McCambridge *(Luz Benedict)*, Chill Wills *(Uncle Bawley)*, Jane Withers *(Vashti Snythe)*, Robert Nichols *(Pinky Snythe)*, Dennis Hopper *(Jordan Benedict III)*, Elsa Cardenas *(Juana)*, Fran Bennett *(Judy Benedict)*, Carroll Baker *(Luz Benedict II)*, Earl Holliman *(Bob Dace)*, Paul Fix *(Dr Horace Lynnton)*, Judith Evelyn *(Mrs Horace Lynnton)*, Carolyn Craig *(Lacey Lynnton)*, Rodney Taylor *(Sir David Karfrey)*, Alexander Scourby *(Old Polo)*, Sal Mineo *(Angel Obregon II)*, Monte Hale *(Bale Clinch)*, Mary Ann Edwards *(Adarene Clinch)*, Napoleon Whiting *(Swazey)*, Charles Watts *(Whiteside)*, Maurice Jara *(Dr Guerra)*, Victor Millan *(Angel Obregon I)*, Pilar Del Rey *(Mrs Obregon)*, Felipe Turich *(Gomez)*, Sheb Wooley *(Gabe Target)*, Francisco Villalobos *(Mexican Priest)*, Ray Whitley *(Watts)*, Tina Menard *(Lupe)*, Anna Maria Majalca *(Petra)*, Mickey Simpson *(Sarge)*, Noreen Nash *(Lona Lane)*, Guy Teague *(Harper)*, Natividad Vacio *(Eusubio)*, Max Terhune *(Dr Walker)*, Ray Bennett *(Dr Borneholm)*, Barbara Barie *(Mary Lou Decker)*, George Dunn *(Vern Decker)*, Slim Talbot *(Clay Hodgins)*, Tex Driscoll *(Clay Hodgins Snr)*, Juney Ellis *(Essie Lou Hodgins)*
Warner Color 198 minutes (modern version usually cut by 20 minutes)
Shot during June–September 1955
Premiered in the USA on 24 November 1956

THE JAMES DEAN STORY (1957)
Produced by George W. George
Directed by Robert Altman
Written by Stewart Stern
Narrated by Martin Gabel
Black and White Length 82 minutes

Bibliography

Alexander, Paul. *James Dean – Boulevard of Broken Dreams*. London: Little, Brown & Company, 1994, Warner Books, 1995.

Astor, Mary. *A Life on Film*. New York: Delacorte Press, 1971.

Bast, William. *James Dean, a Biography*. New York: Ballantine Books, 1956.

Carey, Gary. *Brando*. New York: Pocket Books, 1973.

Ciment, Michel. *Kazan on Kazan*. Cinema One Series. London: Secker & Warburg in association with the British Film Institute, 1973.

Corley, Edwin. *Farewell, My Slightly Tarnished Hero*. London: Michael Joseph, 1973.

de Becker, Raymond. *De Tom Mix à James Dean*. Paris: Librairie Arthème Fayard, 1959.

Dalton, David. *James Dean: The Mutant King*. London: Plexus Publishing Ltd., 1983.

DeVillers, Marceau. *James Dean*. Paris: Anthologie du Cinéma. l'Avant Scène du Cinéma, 1966.

Dos Passos, John. *Mid-Century*. Boston: Houghton Mifflin, 1960.

Ellis, Royston. *Rebel*. Manchester: Consul Edition, World Distributors, 1962.

Gow, Gordon. *Hollywood in the Fifties*. The International Film Guide Series, London: The Tantivy Press, 1971.

Hall, Stuart & Whannel, Paddy. *The Popular Arts*. London: Hutchinson, 1964.

Hardin, Nancy & Schlossberg, Marilyn (eds). *Easy Rider*. New York: Signet, 1969.

Herndon, Venable. *James Dean: A Short Life*. Future Publications Ltd., 1974.

Holley, Val. *James Dean: The Biography*. London: Robson Books Ltd., 1995.

Hopper, Hedda & Brough, James. *The Whole Truth and Nothing But*. New York: Doubleday, 1963.

Hopkins, Jerry. *Elvis, a Biography*. New York: Simon & Schuster, 1971.

Hyams, Joe & Jay. *James Dean: Little Boy Lost*. London: Century Random House, 1992 and Arrow Books Ltd., 1994.

Jordan, Rene. *Marlon Brando*. New York: Pyramid, 1973.

Lindner, Robert M. *Rebel Without a Cause*. New York: Grove Press, 1945.

McCann, Dyer Richard. *Hollywood in Transition*. Boston: Houghton Mifflin, 1962.

McLuhan, Marshall. *The Medium is the Massage*. New York: Random House, 1967.

Martinetti, Ronald. *The James Dean Story*. London: Michael O'Mara Books Ltd., 1995.

Mitgang, H. *Fabulous Yesterday*. New York: Harper, 1961.

Morella, Joe & Epstein, Edward. *The Rebel Hero in Films*. New York: Citadel, 1971.

Morella, Joe & Epstein, Edward. *Brando, the Unauthorised Biography*. London: Thomas Nelson, 1973.

Morin, Edgar. *The Stars*. London: John Calder, 1960.

Newquist, Roy. *Showcase*. New York: William Morrow, 1966.

Richie, Donald. *George Stevens: An American Romantic*. New York: The Museum of Modern Art, 1970.

Ross, Walter. *The Immortal*. London: Frederick Muller, 1958.

Salgues, Yves. *James Dean ou le mal de vivre*. Paris: Pierre Horay, 1957.

Scaduto, Anthony. *Bob Dylan*. London: W. H. Allen, 1972.

Spoto, Donald. *The Life and Legend of James Dean*. Harper Collins, 1996.

Steinbeck, John. *East of Eden*. London: William Heinemann, 1952.

Taylor, Elizabeth. *An Informal Memoir*. New York: Harper & Row, 1965.

Thomas, Bob. *Brando: Portrait of the Rebel as an Artist*. London: W.H. Allen, 1973.

Quirk, Lawrence J. *The Films of Paul Newman*. New York: Citadel, 1971.